Bible Word Search
Volume I

Bible Basics
formerly called
Extracts from the Bible

Compiled by Akili Kumasi

GOD IS LOVE

GIL PUBLICATIONS
THE GOD IS LOVE MINISTRIES
P. O. Box 80275, Brooklyn, NY 11208
www.GILpublications.com
www.BibleWordSearchPuzzles.com

Bible Word Search,
Volume I: Bible Basics
(formerly called - Extracts from the Bible)

Compiled by Akili Kumasi

ISBN-13: 978-0962603501
ISBN-10: 0962603503

THIS IS A WITNESSING and BIBLE STUDY TOOL!

GIL PUBLICATIONS
THE GOD IS LOVE MINISTRIES
P. O. Box 80275, Brooklyn, NY 11208
info@BibleWordSearchPuzzles.com
www.BibleWordSearchPuzzles.com

Bible Word Search Volume I

Bible Basics

Table of Contents

GIL Publications, P. O. Box 80275, Brooklyn, NY 11208
www.BibleWordSearchPuzzles.com

1. Bible Books
First Books Old Testament

<u>Pentateuch</u>
Genesis
Exodus
Leviticus
Numbers
Deuteronomy

<u>History</u>
Joshua
Judges
Ruth
Samuel
Kings
Chronicles
Ezra
Nehemiah
Esther

<u>Poetry</u>
Job
Psalms
Proverbs
Ecclesiastes
Songs of Solomon

GIL Publications, P. O. Box 80275, Brooklyn, NY 11208
www.BibleWordSearchPuzzles.com

```
H  N  E  J  L  N  U  M  B  E  R  S  M  R  J
T  S  E  X  U  E  J  O  K  I  H  B  O  J  P
O  C  O  H  O  D  U  K  Z  U  O  H  I  S  E
D  H  P  N  E  D  G  M  V  H  N  F  A  S  S
Y  R  R  Z  G  M  U  E  A  I  T  L  T  E  G
M  O  O  V  A  S  I  S  S  S  M  H  T  R  E
O  N  V  V  G  I  S  A  N  S  E  S  I  U  N
N  C  E  M  L  L  J  O  H  R  A  V  W  T  E
O  I  R  F  C  K  U  K  L  I  T  O  X  H  S
R  L  B  M  D  O  I  J  S  O  N  P  M  G  I
E  E  S  T  D  N  O  E  Y  S  M  Z  I  Y  S
T  S  P  X  G  S  L  E  X  L  I  O  I  V  D
U  X  A  S  H  C  M  O  U  C  L  Z  N  E  N
E  R  Q  U  C  E  Z  R  A  R  S  T  Q  C  V
D  C  A  E  L  E  V  I  T  I  C  U  S  Q  D
```

1. Bible Books First Books - Old Testament

CHRONICLES	JOB	NUMBERS
DEUTERONOMY	JOSHUA	PROVERBS
ECCLESIASTES	JUDGES	PSALMS
EZRA	KINGS	RUTH
ESTHER	LEVITICUS	SAMUEL
EXODUS	NEHEMIAH	SONGSSOLOMON
GENESIS		

2. Bible Books
Prophecy Books Old Testament

<u>Prophecy</u>
Isaiah
Jeremiah
Lamentations
Ezekiel
Daniel
Hosea
Joel
Amos
Obadiah
Micah
Habakkuk
Zephaniah
Haggai
Zechariah
Malachi

```
Z Y J H H Q Z G G H A I A S I
E K I A P A Z N F W N I H L J
P P R G G W C E P Q O Z A O F
H C T G W H O I C O P M E D W
A B K A A H L D M H E L I Q D
N S I I C H P O F N A N I D I
I K H T Q R S L T V A R R J L
A U C L G A M A I Y G M I B I
H K A G W N T Q E Z K H O A G
N K L N S I O K X Q Q H U S H
M A A E O A D F E P W J B U J
V B M N E J O B I L E I N A D
A A S S E E W O H A I D A B O
D H O H U P U W L E I K E Z E
E H J E R E M I A H O B P I J
```

2. Bible Books – Prophecy Books in OT

AMOS	HOSEA	MALACHI
DANIEL	ISAIAH	MICAH
EZEKIEL	JEREMIAH	OBADIAH
HABAKKUK	JOEL	ZECHARIAH
HAGGAI	LAMENTATIONS	ZEPHANIAH

3. Bible Books
New Testament

Matthew
Mark
Luke
John
Acts
Romans
Corinthians
Galatians
Ephesians
Philippians
Colossians
Thessalonians
Timothy
Titus
Philemon
Hebrews
James
Peter
Revelations

GIL Publications, P. O. Box 80275, Brooklyn, NY 11208
www.BibleWordSearchPuzzles.com

Z Y J H H Q Z G G H A I A S I
E K I A P A Z N F W N I H L J
P P R G G W C E P Q O Z A O F
H C T G W H O I C O P M E D W
A B K A A H L D M H E L I Q D
N S I I C H P O F N A N I D I
I K H T Q R S L T V A R R J L
A U C L G A M A I Y G M I B I
H K A G W N T Q E Z K H O A G
N K L N S I O K X Q Q H U S H
M A A E O A D F E P W J B U J
V B M N E J O B I L E I N A D
A A S S E E W O H A I D A B O
D H O H U P U W L E I K E Z E
E H J E R E M I A H O B P I J

2. Bible Books – Prophecy Books in OT

AMOS	HOSEA	MALACHI
DANIEL	ISAIAH	MICAH
EZEKIEL	JEREMIAH	OBADIAH
HABAKKUK	JOEL	ZECHARIAH
HAGGAI	LAMENTATIONS	ZEPHANIAH

3. Bible Books
New Testament

Matthew
Mark
Luke
John
Acts
Romans
Corinthians
Galatians
Ephesians
Philippians
Colossians
Thessalonians
Timothy
Titus
Philemon
Hebrews
James
Peter
Revelations

```
W S V H S N O I T A L E V E R
X E N Q N S N A I T A L A G J
V E H A N B L V N C I R M A T
S P M T I L W D T J H A M I L
N H D S T N G S A R C E M F U
A E T R H A O M J O S O V E K
I S P O I V M L R F T C O H E
P I N H O J H I A H D U K O P
P A G P L V N S Y S U P O E K
I N W D Z T W Z Y R S X T D E
L S T Y H E S I T O O E K P D
I F N I R U M A R K R M H C G
H U A B T I V U A B U N A T R
P N E I Q N O M E L I H P N R
S H T C O L O S S I A N S N S
```

3. Bible Books - New Testament

ACTS	JOHN	PHILIPPIANS
COLOSSIANS	LUKE	REVELATIONS
CORINTHIANS	MARK	ROMANS
EPHESIANS	MATTHEW	THESSALONIANS
GALATIANS	PETER	TIMOTHY
HEBREWS	PHILEMON	TITUS
JAMES		

4. Women in the Bible

Bathsheba (2 Samuel 11)
Deborah (Judges 4-5)
Delilah (Judges 16)
Dinah – Jacob's Daughter (Genesis 30:21)
Elizabeth (Luke 1:41)
Esther (Esther)
Euodias & Syntche (Philippians 4:2)
Eve (Genesis 2)
Hagar (Genesis 16)
Joanna, Susanna and Mary Magdalene (Luke 8:1-3)
Keturah (Genesis 25:1)
Leah (Genesis 29)
Lot's Wife (Genesis 19:26)
Martha and Mary (Luke 10:38-42)
Mary (Luke 1:26-56)
Miriam (Exodus 15:20)
Moses' Mother (Exodus 2)
Naomi (Ruth 1-4)
Potiphar's Wife (Genesis 39)
Queen of Sheba (1 Kings 10:1-13)
Rachel (Genesis 29)
Rebekah (Genesis 24)
Rehab (Joshua 2:1-24, 6:17)
Ruth (Ruth)
Sapphira (Acts 5)
Sarah (Genesis 12:23)
Widow of Zarephath (1 Kings 17:7-24)
Woman at the Well (John 4)
Woman with the Issue of Blood (Luke 8:43-48)
Zipporah – Moses' Wife (Exodus 2)

```
H A R A B E H S H T A B N A M
H A X E E U O D I A S A H A W
R A R N H R U T H J O T I A Z
Q E L O R A U M F M R R E Z A
U A B I B S B S I A I I C I R
E R W E L E L Q M M D Y M P E
E I E N K E D J O A N N A P P
N H L E P A D D O O L B R O H
S P L V Q H H D I N A H Y R A
H P Y E A R E S T H E R W A T
E A M G A E L I Z A B E T H H
B S A C S A R A H A R U T E K
A R H J R E H T O M S E S O M
K E H A E L L O T S W I F E O
L P O T I P H A R S W I F E T
```

4. Women in the Bible

BATHSHEBA	JOANNA	QUEENSHEBA
BLOOD	KETURAH	RACHEL
DEBORAH	LEAH	REBEKAH
DELILAH	LOTSWIFE	REHAB
DINAH	MARTHA	RUTH
ELIZABETH	MARY	SAPPHIRA
EUODIAS	MIRIAM	SARAH
ESTHER	MOSESMOTHER	WELL
EVE	NAOMI	ZAREPHATH
HAGAR	POTIPHARSWIFE	ZIPPORAH

5. Men in the Old Testament

Aaron
Abel
Abraham
Adam
Cain
Celeb
David
Elijah
Elisha
Enoch
Gideon
Isaac
Ishmael
Jacob
Jehoshaphat
Jesse
Jethro
Jonah
Joseph
Joshua
Lot
Melchizedek
Moses
Noah
Samson
Saul
Solomon

```
J  G  E  M  T  N  G  J  M  Z  V  H  A  O  N
A  O  I  L  A  A  O  B  O  U  M  R  T  O  L
D  I  S  D  I  H  H  S  H  N  S  Z  J  Y  G
A  S  D  E  E  J  A  P  M  K  A  L  T  K  K
M  A  A  Y  P  O  A  R  A  A  H  H  Z  E  W
H  A  V  W  H  H  N  H  B  H  S  C  D  X  X
Z  C  I  M  C  E  C  F  P  A  S  E  O  A  R
H  L  D  C  J  I  Z  S  M  M  Z  O  O  N  I
S  A  U  L  H  I  P  I  O  I  S  A  H  W  E
C  P  H  V  N  Q  E  S  H  O  H  O  A  E  Z
B  D  G  B  I  L  E  C  L  S  R  U  N  E  J
E  E  P  L  A  S  L  O  I  H  H  O  S  I  L
L  X  E  E  C  E  M  L  T  S  R  S  R  D  E
E  Y  D  B  M  O  E  E  O  A  E  P  P  V  U
C  T  Q  A  N  W  J  J  A  J  O  A  O  N  H
```

5. Men in the Old Testament

AARON	ENOCH	JOSHUA
ABEL	GIDEON	LOT
ABRAHAM	ISAAC	MELCHIZEDEK
ADAM	JEHOSHAPHAT	MOSES
CAIN	JESSE	NOAH
CELEB	JETHRO	SAMSON
DAVID	JONAH	SAUL
ELIJAH	JOSEPH	SOLOMON
ELISHA		

6. Men in the Gospels

Barabbas (Matthew 27:16)
Bartimaeus (Mark 10:46)
Caesar (Mark 12:17)
Caiaphas (Matthew 26:57)
Centurion (Matthew 8:5)
Demon possessed man (Luke 8)
Herod (Mark 6:22)
John the Baptist (Matthew 3)
Joseph (Jesus' Step-Father)
Lazarus (Luke 16:19; John 11:1-44)
Levi (Mark 2:13, Luke 5:27)
Nicodemus (John 3:1)
Paralytic (Matthew 9:2)
Pilate (Matthew 27:13)
Rich Man and Lazarus (Luke 16:19)
Simeon (Luke 2:34)
Simon from Cyrene (Luke 23:26)
Simon the Leper (Matthew 26:6)
Wise Men (Matthew 2:1)
Zacchaeus (Luke 19:1-10)
Zechariah (Luke 1:13)

```
K J Q S A H P A I A C J R U P
Z F W W I S E M E N O A D U A
E R C Y R E N E Q H S S E S R
C I J U G Z T O N E I J M U A
H C N E K A F B A M Q E O E L
A H S E O S A C E H E G N A Y
R M P G W P U O L E V I M H T
I A J L T H N E B Y S P A C I
A N B I P F X A A V B I N C C
H P S E S I K S P M W L N A D
P T S L R E P E L T I A C Z Z
A O O Q S U R A Z A L T J O A
J X B A R A B B A S A E R L T
N I C O D E M U S G H I T A H
H E R O D N O I R E T N E C B
```

6. Men in the Gospels

BARABBAS	HEROD	PARALYTIC
BARTIMAEUS	JOHNBAPTIST	PILATE
CAESAR	JOSEPH	RICHMAN
CAIAPHAS	LAZARUS	SIMEON
CENTERION	LEPER	WISEMEN
CYRENE	LEVI	ZACCHAEUS
DEMONMAN	NICODEMUS	ZECHARIAH

7. Jesus' Ministry

The <u>Spirit</u> of the <u>Lord</u> is upon me, because he hath <u>anointed</u> me to <u>preach</u> the <u>gospel</u> to the <u>poor</u>; he hath sent me to <u>heal</u> <u>brokenhearted</u>, to preach <u>deliverance</u> to the <u>captives</u>, and to <u>set</u> at <u>liberty</u> them that are <u>bruised</u>. To preach the <u>acceptable</u> year of the Lord. (Luke 4:18-19 KJV)

...I came that they might have <u>life</u>, and that they might have it <u>more</u> <u>abundantly</u>. (John 10:10 KJV)

I have <u>come</u> into the world as a <u>light</u>, so that no one who believes in me should stay in darkness. (John 12:46 NIV)

For <u>God</u> so <u>loved</u> the world, that he <u>gave</u> his only <u>begotten</u> <u>Son</u>, that whosoever <u>believeth</u> in him should not <u>perish</u>, but have <u>everlasting</u> life. For God sent not his Son into the world to condemn the <u>world</u>; but that the world through him might be <u>saved</u>. (John 3:16-17 KJV)

```
C K S G N I T S A L R E V E S
D O H E H T E V E I L E B P Y
B E N C C M A E R O M B I T D
A R T D A V P N O S T R R E A
B C O N E E G O D W I E I D C
U A Q K I M R H N T B S E S C
N P P Y E O N P D I U L M E E
D T C T K N N E L R I A N T P
A I L A E H H A B V L I F E T
N V K R L W P E E G L Z G T A
T E L D O E D R A S O I X L B
L S R R R E A V L R A S G U L
Y O L I V N E M O C T V P H E
L D S O C O F R O O P E E E T
P H L E B E G O T T E N D D L
```

7. Jesus' Ministry

ABUNDANTLY	DELIVERANCE	MORE
ACCEPTABLE	EVERLASTING	PERISH
ANOINTED	GOD	POOR
BEGOTTEN	GOSPEL	PREACH
BELIEVETH	HEAL	SAVED
BROKENHEARTED	LIBERTY	SET
BRUISED	LIFE	SON
CAPTIVES	LIGHT	SPIRIT
COME	LORD	WORLD
CONDEMN	LOVED	

8. Parables in the Gospels

Wise and Foolish <u>Builders</u> (Matt. 7:24-27)

New wine in old wine <u>skins</u> (Matt. 9:16-17)

The <u>sower</u> and the seed (Mark 4:1-20)

<u>Weeds</u> (Matt. 13:24-30, 36-43)

<u>Mustard</u> Seed (Matt. 13:31-32)

The Lost <u>Sheep</u> (Matt. 18:12-14)

<u>Unmerciful</u> Servant (Matt. 18:21-35)

<u>Workers</u> in the <u>Vineyard</u> (Matt. 20:1-16)

<u>Prodigal</u> (Lost) Son (Luke 15:11-32))

<u>Fig Tree</u> (Matt. 24:32-35)

Shrewd <u>Manager</u> (Luke 16:1-9)

<u>Talents</u> (Matt. 25:14-30)

Ten <u>Virgins</u> (Matt. 25:1-13)

<u>Good Samaritan</u> (Luke 10:25-37)

<u>Friend</u> at <u>Midnight</u> (Luke 11:5-13)

The <u>Great Banquet</u> (Luke 14:15-24

<u>Lost Coin</u> (Luke 15:8-10)

<u>Rich</u> man and Lazarus (Luke 16:19-31)

<u>Persistent Widow</u> (Luke 18:1-8)

```
Z  N  S  S  V  I  N  E  Y  A  R  D  F  X  C
B  R  A  H  O  P  A  P  R  E  G  A  N  A  M
U  K  K  T  E  W  W  S  T  N  E  L  A  T  M
I  X  T  U  I  E  E  O  D  I  H  N  Q  G  S
L  H  E  O  N  R  P  R  D  L  O  S  T  D  G
D  J  C  G  W  M  A  L  X  I  J  T  E  R  P
E  S  T  H  O  L  E  M  A  B  W  E  E  E  D
R  T  L  J  R  C  D  R  A  I  W  A  R  V  N
S  H  A  T  K  F  I  G  C  S  T  S  A  F  E
S  G  G  E  E  Z  A  T  C  I  I  G  H  J  I
H  I  I  U  R  F  R  O  S  S  F  C  O  O  R
R  N  D  Q  S  E  I  N  T  V  I  U  S  O  F
E  D  O  N  E  N  I  E  Y  R  C  D  L  U  D
W  I  R  A  P  K  N  V  I  R  G  I  N  S  E
D  M  P  B  S  T  M  U  S  T  A  R  D  A  H
```

8. Parables in the Gospels

BANQUET	MIDNIGHT	SOWER
BUILDERS	MUSTARD	TALENTS
COIN	PERSISTENT	TREE
FIG	PRODIGAL	UNMERCIFUL
FRIEND	RICH	VINEYARD
GOOD	SAMARITAN	VIRGINS
GREAT	SHEEP	WEEDS
LOST	SHREWD	WIDOW
MANAGER	SKINS	WORKERS

9. Places in the Holy Land

Bethany (John 11:1)
Bethpage (Mark 11:1)
Bethsaida (Mark 8:22)
Caesarea Philippi (Mark 8:27)
Cana (John 2:1)
Capernaum (Matthew 8:5)
Dalmanutha (Mark 8:10)
Decapolis (Mark 7:31)
Galilee (Matthew 2:22)
Gennesaret (Mark 6:53)
Gerasenes (Mark 5:1)
Gethsemane (Matthew 26:36)
Golgotha (Matthew (27:32)
Jerusalem (Matthew 2:1)
Judea (Matthew 2:1)
Korazin (Luke 10:13)
Mount of Olives (Luke 21:37)
Nazareth (Matthew 2:23)
Sumaria (Luke 17:11)
Tyre and Sidon (Mark 3:8)

Y	E	R	Y	T	T	E	R	A	S	E	N	N	E	G
E	N	D	E	C	A	P	O	L	I	S	C	S	M	B
D	I	A	A	A	E	R	A	S	E	A	C	O	F	U
H	W	N	H	H	L	Q	O	H	X	T	U	P	J	W
M	E	A	L	T	T	N	Z	C	A	N	A	H	S	E
U	G	Z	E	T	E	U	I	W	T	V	E	I	E	N
A	A	A	O	Y	T	B	N	O	R	N	D	L	N	A
N	P	R	I	H	X	A	L	A	Q	V	U	I	E	M
R	H	E	S	U	I	I	E	K	M	W	J	P	S	E
E	T	T	M	R	V	E	E	K	O	L	Y	P	A	S
P	E	H	A	E	L	K	J	V	R	R	A	I	R	H
A	B	M	S	I	S	I	D	O	N	J	A	D	E	T
C	U	B	L	G	O	L	G	O	T	H	A	Z	G	E
S	X	A	J	E	R	U	S	A	L	E	M	L	I	G
F	G	B	K	F	A	D	I	A	S	H	T	E	B	N

9. Places in the Holy Land

BETHANY	GALILEE	KORAZIN
BETHPAGE	GENNESARET	MOUNTOLIVES
BETHSAIDA	GERASENES	NAZARETH
CAESAREA	GETHSEMANE	PHILIPPI
CANA	GOLGOTHA	SIDON
CAPERNAUM	JERUSALEM	SUMARIA
DALMANUTHA	JUDEA	TYRE
DECAPOLIS		

10. Jesus Heals

… and they brought unto [H]im all sick people that were taken with divers <u>diseases</u> and <u>torments,</u> and those which were <u>possessed</u> with devils, and those which were <u>lunatic,</u> and those that had the <u>palsy;</u> and [H]e healed them. (Matt. 4:24 KJV)

… and people brought to [H]im all who were ill with various diseases, those <u>suffering</u> severe <u>pain,</u> the <u>demon</u>-possessed, those having <u>seizures,</u> and the <u>paralyzed,</u> and [H]e healed them. (Matt. 4:24 NIV)

Ten men with <u>leprosy</u> (Luke 17:11-19)

Woman with the <u>issue</u> of <u>Blood</u> (Matt. 9:20)

Peter's <u>mother</u>-in-<u>law</u> (Matt.8:14)

Paralytic Man (Matt. 9:2)

Dead <u>Girl</u> (Matt. 9:18)

<u>Blind</u> man (Matt. 9:27)

<u>Deaf</u> and <u>Mute</u> man (Matt. 9:32, Mark 7:31-37)

<u>Canaanite</u> woman's <u>daughter</u> (Matt. 15:21-28)

Man of the <u>Tombs</u> (Graveyard) (Mark 5:1-20)

<u>Crippled</u> Woman healed on the <u>Sabbath</u> (Luke 13:10-17)

Raised Lazarus from the <u>dead</u> (John 11:1-44)

Centurion's son (Luke 7:1-10)

```
Y  B  D  A  U  G  H  T  E  R  X  W  D  C  M
P  S  L  S  K  E  K  N  I  A  P  E  I  O  M
O  S  O  O  B  Y  B  S  N  E  M  T  T  T  D
S  E  C  R  O  M  I  V  T  O  A  H  P  O  I
S  I  Y  A  P  D  O  U  N  N  E  S  H  R  D
E  Z  B  O  N  E  M  T  U  R  W  S  G  M  E
S  U  B  X  Y  A  L  L  I  O  I  A  N  E  L
S  R  G  P  R  P  A  N  C  S  H  D  I  N  P
E  E  B  J  A  R  L  N  S  S  D  N  X  T  P
D  S  R  L  K  A  D  U  I  A  R  I  U  S  I
Q  M  S  Y  W  D  E  A  F  T  B  L  P  J  R
Y  Y  H  T  T  L  R  I  G  B  E  B  D  R  C
U  Q  T  T  S  E  S  A  E  S  I  D  A  K  I
G  K  S  U  F  F  E  R  I  N  G  R  B  T  O
B  T  P  G  H  D  E  Z  Y  L  A  R  A  P  H
```

10.Jesus Heals

BLIND	GIRL	PARALYZED
BLOOD	ISSUE	POSSESSED
CANAANITE	LEPROSY	SABBATH
CRIPPLED	LUNATIC	SEIZURES
DAUGHTER	MOTHERINLAW	SUFFERING
DEAF	MUTE	TOMBS
DEMON	PAIN	TORMENTS
DISEASES	PALSY	

11. Love Is

Love is patient,
Love is kind,
It does not envy,
It does not boast,
It is not proud.
It is not rude,
It is not self-seeking,
It is not easily angered,
It keeps no record of wrongs.
Love does not delight in evil
But rejoices with the truth.
It always protects,
Always trusts,
Always hopes,
Always perseveres.
Love never fails.
(1 Corinthians 13:4-8a NIV)

God Is Love. (1 John 4:8, 16)

Perfect Love Drives Out Fear. (1 John 4:18)

```
K L D R I V E S Y P T S P D O
T I I I D L K V E S P W E E D
R E N V Y H N R A E X R R L C
U J C D E E S O E B I O F I Q
S F P P G E B K U B D N E G D
T I I Z V N F P O A F G C H S
S Q D E H R I A R R L S T T S
Z G R O U F W K I O E I P S E
O E P D W U S O E L U V Z Z C
S E E G J A I J N E S D R O I
S H T Y D R O C E R S G J V O
E A S I L Y C G Z W Z F T W J
P A T I E N T M Y I V X L W E
M P I W E W D E R E G N A E R
P R O T E C T S Y J Z I B K S
```

11.Love Is

ANGERED
BOAST
DELIGHT
DRIVES
EASILY
ENVY
EVIL
FAILS

PROTECTS
HOPES
KEEPS
KIND
PATIENT
PERFECT
PERSEVERES

PROUD
RECORD
REJOICES
RUDE
SELFSEEKING
TRUSTS
WRONGS

12. The Beatitudes

Blessed are the <u>poor</u> in spirit: for theirs is the <u>Kingdom</u> of Heaven

Blessed are they that <u>mourn</u>: for they shall be <u>comforted</u>.

Blessed are the <u>meek</u>: for they shall <u>inherit</u> the <u>earth</u>.

Blessed are they which do <u>hunger</u> and <u>thirst</u> after <u>righteousness</u>: for they shall be <u>filled</u>.

Blessed are the <u>merciful</u>: for they shall <u>obtain</u> <u>mercy</u>.

Blessed are the <u>pure</u> in heart: for they shall see God.

Blessed are the <u>peacemakers</u>: for they shall be called the <u>children</u> of God.

Blessed are they which are <u>persecuted</u> for righteousness' sake: for theirs is the kingdom of Heaven.

Blessed are ye, when men shall <u>revile</u> you, and persecute you, and shall say all <u>manner</u> of evil against you <u>falsely</u>, for my <u>sake</u>.

Matthew 5:3-11 KJV

```
F  R  N  M  C  H  I  L  D  R  E  N  E  H  B
P  A  I  E  E  M  E  E  K  T  A  V  U  L  D
E  T  L  G  V  R  X  P  L  R  R  N  X  E  E
R  Y  S  S  H  A  C  G  O  Z  G  F  L  A  D
S  L  P  R  E  T  E  Y  E  E  P  L  R  P  S
E  U  O  O  I  L  E  H  R  E  I  T  S  U  E
C  F  O  N  U  H  Y  O  A  F  H  P  H  R  U
U  I  R  S  A  Y  T  C  U  M  W  R  W  E  N
T  C  J  E  E  N  E  T  M  S  A  J  W  X  R
E  R  X  X  I  M  I  T  R  O  N  N  J  L  U
D  E  Q  A  A  R  I  G  K  E  D  E  N  M  O
V  M  T  K  E  R  I  D  I  D  V  G  S  E  M
N  B  E  H  I  S  A  K  E  C  E  I  N  S  R
O  R  N  P  M  L  Z  S  J  R  I  K  L  I  P
S  I  S  Y  D  E  T  R  O  F  M  O  C  E  K
```

12. The Beatitudes

CHILDREN	KINGDOM	PERSECUTED
COMFORTED	MANNER	POOR
EARTH	MEEK	PURE
FALSELY	MERCIFUL	REVILE
FILLED	MERCY	RIGHTEOUSNESS
HEAVEN	MOURN	SAKE
HUNGER	OBTAIN	SPIRIT
INHERIT	PEACEMAKERS	THIRST

13. The Apostles

Simon - Son of John - Jesus named him <u>Peter</u> (Mark 3:16) or
    <u>Cephas</u> (John 1:42) which means a <u>stone</u>. He was a
    <u>Fisherman</u>.

<u>Andrew</u> - aka <u>Levi</u>

<u>James</u> - Son of <u>Zebedee</u>

<u>John</u> - James brother. - The one whom Jesus loved. (John 20:2;
    21:20) - Jesus named him <u>Boanerges</u> which means son of
    <u>thunder</u>. (Mark 3:17)

<u>Philip</u>

<u>Bartholomew</u> - <u>Nathanael</u>-the true Israelite in whom there is
    nothing <u>false</u>. (John 1:45-46)

<u>Matthew</u> - <u>Tax</u> <u>collector</u>.

<u>Thomas</u> - called <u>Didymus</u> (John 20:24)

James - Son of <u>Alphaeus</u>

<u>Simon</u> - called the <u>Zealot</u>

<u>Judas</u> - Son of James (Luke 6:16)

Judas <u>Iscariot</u> - became the <u>traitor</u>

<u>Matthias</u> - replaced Judas Iscariot (Acts 1:12-26)

<u>Paul</u> - <u>Saul</u> of <u>Tarsus</u> (Act 9:11, 1-19)

Other references:
Matt. 10:1-4; 9:9
Mark 3:13-19
Luke 6:12-16
John 1:35-51

```
M T Z S S U E A H P L A R T I
R A A E I A K N H O J E H S A
F O T X A M Z D C S T O N N
I S T T C L O G M E M H D W A
S A L I H O O N P A U R E Z T
H I L B A E L T S N E M T E H
E H X I S R W L D W O N L B A
R T P A U L T E E L N D U E N
M T X D E O R D O C J H A D A
A A C N S P I H T S T U S E E
N M O E H D T C A A A O D E L
F T M I Y R U C F V R H R A M
S A L M A M Z I V E L S P D S
J I U B T O I R A C S I U E V
P S B O A N E R G E S L Q S C
```

13. The Apostles

ALPHAEUS	JUDAS	SIMON
ANDREW	LEVI	STONE
BARTHOLOMEW	MATTHEW	TARSUS
BOANERGES	MATTHIAS	TAXCOLLECTOR
CEPHAS	NATHANAEL	THOMAS
DIDYMUS	PAUL	THUNDER
FISHERMAN	PETER	TRAITOR
ISCARIOT	PHILIP	ZEALOT
JAMES	SAUL	ZEBEDEE
JOHN		

14. Our Position in the Kingdom of God

Aliens and Strangers on earth   (Hebrews 11:13 NIV)
Ambassadors for Reconciliation   (2 Corinthians 5:20)
Believers   (1 Timothy 4:12, Acts 5:14)
Born Again   (John 3:3, 7)
Brethern   (Romans 8:29 KJV)
Brothers   (Romans 8:29 NIV)
Children of God   (Romans 8:16)
Chosen and Ordained   (John 15:16, 19)
Citizens of Heaven   (Philippians 3:20 NIV; Luke 10:20 TLB)
Co-Heirs with Christ   (Romans 8:17 NIV)
Friends   (John 15:14-15)
Heirs of God   (Romans 8:17)
His Workmanship   (Ephesians 2:10)
Joint Heirs   (Romans 8:17 KJV)
More Than Conquerors   (Romans 8:37)
New Creatures   (2 Corinthians 5:17)
Saints   (1 Corinthians 1:2)
Saved   (John 3:17)
Soldiers of Jesus Christ   (2 Timothy 2:3-4)
Sons of God   (Romans 8:23 NIV)
Souls   (1 Peter 3:20)
Spiritual   (Galatians 6:1)
Strangers and Pilgrims on earth   (Hebrews 11:13 KJV)
Vessels unto Honor   (2 Timothy 2:20-21)
Victors   (1 Corinthians 15:57)
Workmanship (Ephesians 2:10)

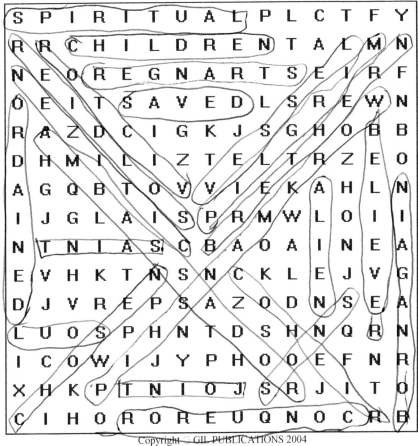

S	P	I	R	I	T	U	A	L	P	L	C	T	F	Y
R	R	C	H	I	L	D	R	E	N	T	A	L	M	N
N	E	O	R	E	G	N	A	R	T	S	E	I	R	F
O	E	I	T	S	A	V	E	D	L	S	R	E	W	N
R	A	Z	D	C	I	G	K	J	S	G	H	O	B	B
D	H	M	L	I	Z	T	E	L	T	R	Z	E	O	
A	G	Q	B	T	O	V	V	I	E	K	A	H	L	N
I	J	G	L	A	I	S	P	R	M	W	L	O	I	I
N	T	N	I	A	S	C	B	A	O	A	I	N	E	A
E	V	H	K	T	N	S	N	C	K	L	E	J	V	G
D	J	V	R	E	P	S	A	Z	O	D	N	S	E	A
L	U	O	S	P	H	N	T	D	S	H	N	Q	R	N
I	C	O	W	I	J	Y	P	H	O	O	E	F	N	R
X	H	K	P	T	N	I	O	J	S	R	J	I	T	O
C	I	H	O	R	O	R	E	U	Q	N	O	C	R	B

14. Our Position in the Kingdom of God

ALIEN
AMBASSADOR
BELIEVER
BORNAGAIN
BRETHERN
CHILDREN
CHOSEN
CITIZEN

COHEIR
CONQUEROR
JOINT
ORDAINED
PILGRIM
SAINT
SAVED
SOLDIER

SONS
SOUL
SPIRITUAL
STRANGER
VESSEL
VICTOR
WORKMANSHIP

GIL Publications, P. O. Box 80275, Brooklyn, NY 11208
www.BibleWordSearchPuzzles.com

15. Gifts of the Spirit

Ephesians 4:11   Apostles
                        Prophets
                        Evangelists
                        Pastors
                        Teachers

Romans 12:6-8   Prophecy
                        Serving
                        Teaching
                        Encouraging
                        Giving
                        Leadership
                        Mercy

I Corinthians 12:8-10   Word of Wisdom
                        Word of Knowledge
                        Faith
                        Gift of Healing
                        Working of Miracles
                        Prophecy
                        Discerning of Spirits
                        Speaking in Tongues
                        Interpretation of Tongues

I Corinthians 12:28   Apostles
                        Prophets
                        Teacher
                        Working of Miracles
                        Healing
                        Helps
                        Government (Administration)
                        Speaking in Tongues
                        Interpretation of Tongues

15.Gifts of the Spirit

APOSTLE	HEALING	PROPHET
DISCERNING	HELPS	SERVING
ENCOURAGING	KNOWLEDGE	SPIRIT
EVANGELIST	LEADERSHIP	TEACHER
FAITH	MERCY	TONGUES
GIVING	MIRACLE	WISDOM
GOVERNMENT	PASTOR	WORD

16. The Full Armor of God

Finally, my brethen, be strong in the Lord, and in the <u>power</u> of [H]is might.

Put on the whole <u>armor</u> of God, that ye may be able to stand against the <u>wiles</u> (<u>schemes</u> -Eph. 6:11-NIV) of the devil.

For we <u>wrestle</u> not against flesh and blood but against <u>principalities</u>, against powers, against the <u>rulers</u> of the darkness of this world, against spiritual <u>wickedness</u> in high places.

Wherefore take unto you the <u>whole</u> armor of God, that ye may be able to stand to <u>withstand</u> in the evil day, having done all, to stand.

Stand, therefore, having your

- loins girt about with <u>truth</u>, and

- having on the <u>breastplate</u> of righteousness; (God's <u>approval</u> - Eph. 6:14-TLB)

- And you <u>feet</u> shod with the preparation of the <u>gospel</u> of <u>peace</u>;

- Above all, taking the <u>shield</u> of faith, wherewith ye shall be able to quench all the fiery <u>darts</u> of the wicked.

- And take the <u>helmet</u> of <u>salvation</u>, and

- the <u>sword</u> of the Spirit, which is the word of God:

<u>Praying</u> always with all prayer and <u>supplication</u> in the Spirit, and watching thereunto with all <u>perseverance</u> and supplication for all saints...

(Ephesians 6:10-18 KJV)

16.The Full Armor of God

APPROVAL	PERSEVERANCE	SWORD
ARMOR	POWER	TRUTH
BREASTPLATE	PRAYING	WHOLE
DARTS	PRINCIPALITIES	WICKEDNESS
FEET	RULERS	WILES
GOSPEL	SALVATION	WITHSTAND
HELMET	SHIELD	WRESTLE
PEACE	SUPPLICATIONS	

17. The Baptism of Jesus

Then Jesus came from Galilee to the Jordan to be baptized by John [The Baptist]. But John tried to deter [H]im, saying, "I need to be baptized by you, and do you come to me?"

Jesus replied, "Let it be so now; it is proper for us to do this to fulfill all righteousness." Then John consented.

As soon as Jesus was baptized, he went up out of the water. At that moment heaven was opened, and [H]e saw the Spirit of God descending like a dove and lighting on [H]im.

And a voice from heaven said, "This is my Son, whom I love, with him I am well pleased."

(Matthew 3:13-17 NIV)

```
D  V  W  A  T  E  R  V  N  O  Z  H  D  F  P
Y  E  O  S  O  N  E  D  G  G  E  E  H  M  M
G  R  T  I  S  W  N  X  N  A  N  B  D  R  N
D  H  I  E  C  G  J  I  V  E  E  E  S  E  J
E  F  Z  G  R  E  D  E  P  W  V  N  G  P  L
S  U  H  G  H  N  N  O  G  O  D  W  M  L  G
A  H  N  D  E  T  C  S  P  I  R  I  T  I  N
E  Y  L  C  J  E  E  O  O  R  R  Q  H  E  I
L  Z  S  E  N  D  N  O  N  T  O  I  M  D  T
P  E  S  I  J  O  H  N  U  S  N  P  M  O  H
D  U  I  L  O  V  E  F  B  S  E  E  E  Q  G
S  O  E  Y  W  E  L  L  A  G  N  N  M  R  I
D  F  U  L  F  I  L  L  O  Z  N  E  T  O  L
G  A  L  I  L  L  E  E  P  U  H  T  S  E  M
G  H  K  N  B  D  E  Z  I  T  P  A  B  S  D
```

17. The Baptism of Jesus

BAPTIZED	HEAVEN	PROPER
CONSENTED	JESUS	REPLIED
DESCENDING	JOHN	RIGHTEOUSNESS
DETER	LIGHTING	SON
DOVE	LOVE	SPIRIT
FULFILL	MOMENT	VOICE
GALILLEE	OPENED	WATER
GOD	PLEASED	WELL

18. Tithes and Offerings

Tithes

    The Melchizedek, king of Salem brought out bread and wine. He was priest of God Most High, and he blessed Abram [Abraham], saying "

    "Blessed be Abram by God Most High,
        Creator of heaven and earth.
    And blessed be God Most High,
        who delivered your enemies into your hand."
Then Abram gave him a tenth of everything. (Genesis 14:18-20 NIV)

    Bring the best of the firstfruits of your soil to the house of the Lord your God. (Exodus 23:19; 34:26 NIV)

    Honor the Lord with thy substance and with the firstfruits of all thine increase: So that thy barns be filled with plenty, and thy presses shall burst out with new wine. (Proverbs 3:9-10 KJV)

    Bring ye all the tithes into the storehouse, that there may be meat in mine house, and prove me now herewith, saith the Lord of hosts, if I will not open you the windows of heaven, and pour you out a blessing, that there shall not be room enough to receive it. (Malachi 3:10 KJV)

Offerings

    Remember this: Whosoever sows sparingly will also reap sparingly, and whosoever sows generously will also reap generously. Each man should give what he has decided in his heart to give, not reluctantly or under compulsion, for God loves a cheerful giver. (2 Cor. 9:6-7 NIV)

```
S  C  H  D  Y  L  G  N  I  R  A  P  S  F  G
P  E  W  O  E  V  I  G  Q  S  T  R  I  N  W
O  H  I  I  U  V  P  O  D  S  E  L  I  S  E
U  E  W  M  N  S  G  K  E  V  L  H  F  U  S
R  I  T  M  E  D  E  B  I  E  T  Z  Y  B  U
Y  N  V  M  E  N  O  G  D  Y  Q  X  I  S  O
O  C  B  P  Q  L  E  W  R  K  I  N  G  T  H
U  R  O  O  M  D  C  E  B  H  I  G  H  A  E
O  E  E  E  H  T  V  H  O  R  E  E  V  N  R
U  A  W  T  S  E  J  T  I  Y  I  H  Z  C  O
T  S  N  E  A  G  N  O  I  Z  T  N  T  E  T
Q  E  I  B  T  V  T  S  O  M  E  N  G  I  S
T  R  R  L  U  F  R  E  E  H  C  D  E  S  T
P  A  F  I  R  S  T  F  R  U  I  T  E  L  S
M  G  E  N  E  R  O  U  S  L  Y  S  J  K  P
```

18.Tithes and Offerings

ABRAM	GIVE	POUR-YOU-OUT
BEST	GIVER	PRIEST
BRING	HIGH	ROOM
CHEERFUL	HOUSE	SPARINGLY
ENEMIES	INCREASE	STOREHOUSE
EVERYTHING	KING	SUBSTANCE
FILLED	MELCHIZEDEK	TENTH
FIRST-FRUIT	MOST	TITHE
GENEROUSLY	PLENTY	WINDOW

19. Humility

The greatest among you will be your servant. For everyone who exalts himself will be humbled, and he who humbles himself will be exalted. (Matthew 23:11-12 NIV)

He guides the humble in what is right and teaches them [H]is way. (Proverb 25:9 NIV)

The meek will [H]e guide in judgment: and the meek will [H]e teach [H]is way. (Proverb 25:9 KJV)

By humility and the fear of the Lord are riches, and honor, and life. (Proverb 22:4 KJV)

…God resisteth the proud, but giveth grace unto the humble. (James 4:6 KJV)

Does not the potter have the right to make of the same lump of clay some pottery for noble purposes and some for common use? (Romans 9:21 NIV)

Let this mind be in you, which was also in Christ Jesus: Who, being in the form of God, thought it not robbery to be equal with God: But made himself of no reputation, and took upon him the form of a servant, and was made in the likeness of men:
And being found in fashion as man, [H]e humbled himself, and became obedient unto death; even the death on the cross.
Wherefore God also hath highly exalted him, and given him a name which is above every name… (Philippians 2:5-9 KJV)

```
G  H  A  T  J  L  D  P  R  O  U  D  B  D  L
R  U  S  N  E  N  U  E  H  U  M  B  L  E  D
E  M  H  S  N  A  M  M  A  O  M  T  A  K  C
A  I  D  S  E  O  C  I  P  T  N  W  U  B  T
T  L  M  G  E  D  M  H  F  O  H  O  V  X  H
E  I  L  E  F  H  I  M  E  U  F  G  R  N  G
S  T  J  T  E  N  C  U  O  S  P  C  O  E  I
T  Y  T  N  A  K  F  I  G  C  E  I  L  W  R
T  M  N  E  R  Y  G  T  R  V  T  T  G  A  P
X  I  E  I  P  L  I  F  E  A  N  T  E  O  Y
T  N  M  D  T  I  X  R  T  A  S  X  T  S  G
C  D  G  E  R  T  Y  U  V  I  A  T  S  R  S
W  A  D  B  I  O  P  R  R  L  E  O  A  O  L
S  H  U  O  N  E  E  H  T  R  R  C  H  R  T
C  J  J  E  R  S  C  S  N  C  E  M  J  Q  M
```

19. Humility

CHRIST	GUIDES	OBEDIENT
COMMON	HONOR	POTTER
CROSS	HUMBLED	PROUD
DEATH	HUMILITY	REPUTATION
EVERYONE	JUDGMENT	RICHES
EXALTS	LIFE	RIGHT
FEAR	LUMPOFCLAY	SERVANT
GRACE	MEEK	TEACHES
GREATEST	MIND	

20. Devils, Demons, Fallen Angels

Abaddon (Revelations 9:11)
Accuser (Revelations 12:10)
Adversary (Psalm 74:10)
Angel of the Abyss (Revelations 9:11 NIV)
Angel of the Bottomless Pit (Revelations 9:11 KJV)
Apollyon (Revelations 9:11)
Avenger (Psalm 8:2 KJV)
Beelzebub, Prince of the devils (Matthew 12:24)
Demons (Matthew 9:33 NIV)
Devil (Luke 8:35 KJV)
Devour (Malachi 3:11)
Enemy (Psalm 8:2)
Evil One (John 17:15 NIV)
Evil Spirit (Acts 19:16)
Father of Lies (John 8:44 NIV)
Foe (Psalm 8:2)
god of the world (2 Corinthians 4:4)
Liar (John 8:44)
Lucifer (Isaiah 14:12)
Murderer (John 8:44)
Prince of the Power of the Air (Ephesians 2:2)
Prince of this world (John 12:31)
Principalities and powers (Romans 8:38)
Roaring Lion (1 Peter 5:8)
Rules of Darkness (Ephesians 6:12)
Satan (Luke 22:31)
Serpent (Genesis 3:4)
Tempter (Matthew 4:3)
Thief (John 10:10)
Unclean Spirit (Luke 11:24)
Wicked One (Matthew 13:19)

```
S  S  F  D  Q  I  O  R  A  I  L  Y  A  J  R
T  P  S  E  F  O  E  M  R  H  R  B  Y  O  D
T  N  I  Y  I  F  S  K  H  A  A  A  A  E  D
U  A  W  R  B  H  J  C  S  D  V  R  K  E  A
R  P  B  C  I  A  T  R  D  E  I  C  W  V  R
E  J  K  U  C  T  E  O  N  N  I  A  S  I  K
R  H  B  X  B  V  N  G  G  W  H  T  D  L  N
E  L  J  S  D  E  E  L  R  M  Y  M  E  N  E
D  G  F  A  D  R  Z  R  U  E  E  W  M  T  S
R  L  M  L  N  P  F  L  E  C  T  U  O  W  S
U  Z  R  A  R  Q  S  N  E  S  I  P  N  R  R
M  O  T  I  M  Z  E  M  R  E  U  F  M  B  G
W  A  N  R  A  G  I  T  I  P  B  C  E  E  X
S  C  P  U  N  C  L  E  A  N  R  B  C  R  T
E  K  T  J  F  N  O  Y  L  L  O  P  A  A  N
```

20.Devils, Demons, Fallen Angels

ABADDON	DEMON	PRINCE
ABYSS	ENEMY	ROARING
ACCUSER	EVIL	SATAN
ADVERSARY	FOE	SPIRIT
AIR	LIAR	TEMPTER
APOLLYON	LIES	THIEF
AVENGER	LUCIFER	UNCLEAN
BEELZEBUB	MURDERER	WICKED
DARKNESS	PIT	WORLD

21.   Hebrews in the Wilderness

But God led the people about, through the way of the wilderness of the Red Sea: and the children of Israel went up harnessed out of the land of Egypt. And Moses took the bones of Joseph with him… (Exodus 13:18-19a KJV)

And the Lord went before them by day in a pillar of a cloud…and by night in a pillar of fire … (Exodus 13:21 KJV)

God Provides

…the Lord shall give you in the evening flesh to eat, and in the morning bread to the full…And it came to pass, that at [eve] the quails came up and covered the camp: and in the morning the dew lay round …and when the dew that lay was gone up, behold, upon the face of the wilderness there lay a small round thing…it is manna… (Exodus 16:8,13-14,15)

Strike the rock, and water will come out of it for the people to drink. (Exodus 17:6b NIV)

The Law

I am thy Lord, Which have brought thee out of Egypt, out of the house of bondage. Thou shall have no other gods before me. [The Ten Commandments] (Exodus 20:1-17)

Moses said to the people, "Do not be afraid. God has come to test you, so that the fear of God will be with you to keep you from sinning." (Exodus 20:20 NIV)

```
E  Z  J  M  A  N  N  A  B  T  Q  A  N  E  Z
L  G  K  O  C  X  K  U  O  P  C  N  L  S  D
X  A  A  W  S  R  T  V  N  Y  D  P  T  I  W
W  G  E  D  I  E  O  W  E  G  O  N  A  S  X
F  D  M  T  N  L  P  K  S  E  E  R  Y  A  D
D  A  E  R  B  O  D  H  P  M  F  P  M  A  C
P  I  L  L  A  R  B  E  D  A  T  E  S  T  P
N  V  J  B  L  C  I  N  R  K  X  I  K  S  R
K  C  O  R  L  S  A  M  G  N  D  Y  E  C  E
R  F  O  O  L  M  O  N  J  N  E  R  H  S  D
Q  C  U  I  M  R  I  W  C  J  I  S  V  W  S
V  D  A  O  N  G  B  B  R  F  S  N  S  H  E
Y  U  C  I  H  G  E  K  I  R  T  S  N  O  A
Q  V  N  T  K  E  E  P  O  M  R  R  W  I  F
C  G  H  A  R  N  E  S  S  E  S  F  H  J  S
```

21.Hebrews in the Wilderness

AFRAID	EGYPT	PILLAR
BONDAGE	FIRE	REDSEA
BONES	HARNESSES	QUAILS
BREAD	JOSEPH	ROCK
CAMP	KEEP	SINNING
CLOUD	MANNA	STRIKE
COMMANDMENTS	MORNING	TEN
DAY	NIGHT	TEST
DEW	PEOPLE	WILDERNESS

22. Hebrews Tested in the Desert

Remember how the Lord our God led you all the way in the desert these forty years, to humble you and to test you in order to know what was in your heart, whether or not you would keep his commands. He humbled you, causing you to hunger and then feeding you with manna ... to teach you that man does not live on bread alone but on every word that comes from the mouth of the Lord. Your clothes did not wear out and your feet did not swell during these forty years. (Deuteronomy 8:2-4 NIV)

If you ever forget the Lord your God and follow other gods and worship and bow down to them, I testify against you today that you will surely be destroyed. Like the nations the Lord destroyed before you, so you will be destroyed for not obeying the Lord your God. (Deuteronomy 8:19-20 NIV)

Worship the Lord your God and his blessing will be on your food and water...I will send terror ahead of you and throw into confusion every nation you encounter. I will make all your enemies turn and run. (Exodus 23:25, 27 NIV)

And all the congregation lifted up their voice and ...murmured against Moses and Aaron...Let us make a captain, and let us return into Egypt... (Numbers 14:1, 2, 4 KJV)

The Lord replied, "I have forgiven them, as you asked. Nevertheless, as surely as I live and as surely as the glory of the Lord fills the whole earth, not one of the men who saw my glory and the miraculous signs I performed in Egypt and in the desert but who disobeyed me and tested me ten times ---not one of them will ever see the land I promised to their forefathers... But because my servant Caleb has a different spirit and follows me wholeheartedly, I will bring him into the land...

(Numbers 14:20-23, 24 NIV)

GIL Publications, P. O. Box 80275, Brooklyn, NY 11208
www.BibleWordSearchPuzzles.com

```
N D T R E T N U O C N E N S N
Y I E E Y D S R A E Y O E O S
M L A S R U E M F N R H I N D
I B D T E R J X H A T T O M E
R O W E P R O A A O A I H O S
A P E X T A T R L G T E F U T
C Y A E U R C C E A U T A T R
U T R C W N A R N T E E F H O
L R B E S R G E G M B D L J Y
O O P E E N R W H N U E H L E
U F M T O E D O B E I R L K D
S O U C G A X R R W L D M A S
C R N N L A N D J Z R O E U C
N U U T E S T I F Y K U H E R
R H F O R E F A T H E R S W F
```

22.Hebrews Tested in the Desert

AARON	FEEDING	NATIONS
CALEB	FEET	RETURN
CAPTAIN	FOREFATHERS	RUN
CLOTHES	FORTY	TERROR
COMES	HUNGER	TESTIFY
CONGREGATION	LAND	WEAR
DESERT	MIRACULOUS	WHOLEHEARTEDLY
DESTROYED	MOUTH	WORD
ENCOUNTER	MURMUR	YEARS

23. Jesus Tempted in the Desert

Then was Jesus <u>led</u> up of the Spirit into the wilderness to be <u>tempted</u> by the devil. And when he had <u>fasted</u> <u>forty</u> <u>days</u> and forty <u>nights</u>, he was afterward an hungered.

And when the <u>tempter</u> came to him, he said, If thou be the Son of God, command that these <u>stones</u> be made bread. But He answered and said, "It is <u>written</u>, Man shall not live by bread alone, but by every word that <u>proceed</u>eth out of the mouth of God."

Then the devil <u>take</u>th him up into the <u>holy</u> <u>city</u>, and setteth him on a <u>pinnacle</u> of the <u>temple</u>. And saith unto him, If thou be the Son of God, <u>cast</u> thyself down: for it is written, He shall give his <u>angels</u> charge concerning thee, and in their hands they shall <u>bear</u> thee up, lest at anytime thou dash thy foot against a stone. Jesus said unto him, "It is written again, Thou shall not tempt the Lord thy God."

Again, the devil taketh him up into an exceeding <u>high</u> <u>mountain</u>, and showeth him all the <u>kingdoms</u> of the <u>world</u>, and the glory of them; And saith unto him, All these things will I give you if thou wilt fall down and worship me. Then saith Jesus unto him, "Get thee <u>hence</u>, Satan; for it is written, Thou shalt <u>worship</u> the Lord they God, and him only shalt thou <u>serve</u>.

Then the devil <u>leave</u>th him, and, behold, angels came and <u>ministered</u> unto him. (Matthew 4:1-11 KJV)

```
T  T  A  K  E  H  O  H  E  F  B  W  M  S  M
N  S  S  E  Z  R  I  X  O  E  O  I  E  G  O
W  A  A  U  S  G  E  R  A  D  N  R  P  S  U
N  K  T  C  H  V  T  R  E  I  V  H  R  W  N
D  V  L  A  A  Y  S  T  S  E  H  N  O  Q  T
A  Y  P  E  S  E  S  T  P  M  R  E  C  E  A
P  Z  L  Q  N  A  E  D  A  Y  S  T  E  L  I
I  B  S  O  F  R  H  C  B  T  G  T  E  C  N
H  O  T  M  E  N  X  E  U  I  J  I  D  A  H
S  S  R  D  O  S  I  E  N  C  W  R  J  N  C
R  L  I  K  G  D  L  G  L  C  D  W  T  N  K
O  J  E  W  F  X  G  E  H  P  E  L  R  I  X
W  I  B  D  W  Z  H  N  G  T  M  D  R  P  V
N  H  O  L  Y  W  D  W  I  N  S  E  X  O  B
T  E  M  P  T  E  D  G  C  K  A  V  T  A  W
```

23. Jesus Tempted in the Desert

ANGELS
BEAR
CAST
CITY
DAYS
FASTED
FORTY
HENCE
HIGH

HOLY
KINGDOMS
LEAVE
LED
MINISTERED
MOUNTAIN
NIGHTS
PINNACLE
PROCEED

SATAN
SERVE
STONES
TAKE
TEMPLE
TEMPTED
WORLD
WORSHIP
WRITTEN

24. Prayer

"And when you pray, do not be like the hypocrites, for they love to pray standing in the synagogues and on the street corners to be seen by men...But when you pray, go into your room, close the door and pray to your Father, who is unseen. Then your Father, who sees what is done in secret, will reward you. And when you pray, do not keep on babbling like pagans, for they think they will be heard because of their many words....for your Father knows what you need before you ask him. (Matthew 6:5-8 NIV)

...Therefore I tell you, whatever you ask for in prayer, believe that you have received it, and it will be yours. And when you stand praying, if you hold anything against anyone, forgive him, so that your Father in heaven may forgive you your sins. (Mark 11:24-25 NIV)

The sacrifice of the wicked is an abomination unto the Lord: but the prayer of the upright is his delight. The Lord is far from the wicked: but he heareth the prayer of the righteous. (Proverb 15:8, 29 KJV)

```
D  G  C  D  E  G  N  I  L  B  B  A  B  C  T
S  E  N  A  R  Y  U  S  Y  A  R  P  V  E  P
Y  T  L  I  N  A  J  N  O  A  T  K  R  A  H
N  G  E  I  H  O  W  I  U  L  J  E  G  E  S
A  E  R  E  G  T  I  E  R  Z  C  A  A  E  T
G  R  E  S  R  H  Y  T  R  S  N  R  T  X  Q
O  O  V  F  U  T  T  N  A  S  D  I  G  I  W
G  F  E  A  H  C  S  Z  A  N  R  R  O  O  M
U  E  T  R  A  E  H  U  T  C  I  M  Q  Z  D
E  R  A  H  Y  N  P  S  O  A  E  M  O  B  M
S  E  H  V  E  R  N  P  R  K  S  S  O  R  K
N  H  W  E  I  I  Y  C  O  I  N  K  O  B  O
S  T  S  G  A  H  R  D  O  K  Q  O  H  L  A
F  N  H  G  S  T  A  N  D  I  N  G  W  I  C
U  T  A  S  A  C  R  I  F  I  C  E  Z  S  M
```

24. Prayer

ABOMINATION	HEAR	SCERET
AGAINST	HEARD	STANDING
ANYTHING	HYPOCRITES	STREET
ASKHIM	KNOWS	SYNAGOGUES
BABBLING	PAGANS	THEREFORE
CLOSE	PRAY	UNSEEN
DELIGHT	REWARD	UPRIGHT
DOOR	ROOM	WHATEVER
FAR	SACRIFICE	YOU

25. Faith

"…If you have <u>faith</u> as a grain of <u>mustard</u> <u>seed</u>, ye shall say unto this mountain, <u>Remove</u> hence to <u>yonder</u> place; and it shall remove; and <u>nothing</u> shall be <u>impossible</u> unto you. (Matthew 17:20 KJV)

So then faith cometh by <u>hearing</u>, and hearing by the word of God. (Romans 10:17 KJV)

For we <u>walk</u> by faith and not by <u>sight</u>… (Romans 5:7 KJV)

Now faith is the <u>substance</u> of <u>things</u> <u>hoped for</u>, the <u>evidence</u> of things <u>not seen</u>. Through faith we <u>understand</u> that the worlds were framed y the word of God, so that things which are seen were not made of things which do appear. (Hebrews 11:1, 3 KJV)

And without faith it is impossible to <u>please</u> God, because anyone who comes to him <u>must</u> <u>believe</u> that he <u>exists</u> and that he <u>rewards</u> those who <u>earnestly</u> <u>seek</u> him. (Hebrews 11:6 NIV)

What good is it, my brother, if a man claims to have faith but has no <u>deeds</u>? Can such faith <u>save</u> him? (James 2:14 NIV)… For as the <u>body</u> without the spirit is <u>dead</u>, so faith without <u>works</u> is dead also. (James 2:26 KJV)

```
D  Y  M  U  S  T  L  E  M  Y  Q  H  L  E  R
E  E  D  S  E  E  K  A  O  Y  E  I  V  E  S
A  Y  E  O  L  K  F  N  N  A  M  I  W  K  T
R  W  K  D  B  U  D  G  R  P  D  A  R  X  P
N  D  K  I  S  E  N  I  O  E  R  O  P  I  R
E  P  N  Y  R  I  N  S  N  D  W  A  L  K  O
S  T  Z  A  H  G  S  C  S  S  D  H  X  V  F
T  W  V  T  T  I  E  N  X  T  I  W  H  H  D
L  Q  O  E  B  S  E  M  O  S  H  G  A  I  E
Y  N  F  L  H  E  R  V  U  T  T  I  H  Y  P
S  W  E  T  V  J  D  E  E  S  S  S  N  T  O
A  Y  I  O  E  P  A  J  D  I  T  E  I  G  H
R  A  M  I  V  D  E  E  S  N  L  A  E  X  S
F  E  Y  D  A  B  D  X  J  Y  U  E  R  N  E
R  S  U  B  S  T  A  N  C  E  P  Q  B  D  C
```

Copyright © GIL PUBLICATIONS 2004

25.Faith

BELIEVE	HOPEDFOR	SEED
BODY	IMPOSSIBLE	SEEK
DEAD	MUST	SIGHT
DEEDS	MUSTARD	SUBSTANCE
EARNESTLY	NOTHING	THINGS
EVIDENCE	NOTSEEN	UNDERSTAND
EXISTS	REMOVE	WALK
FAITH	REWARDS	WORKS
HEARING	SAVE	YONDER

26. The Fall of Jericho

Now <u>Jericho</u> was straitly shut up because of the <u>children</u> of <u>Israel</u>: none went out, and none came in. And the Lord said unto Joshua, See, I have given into thine <u>hand</u> Jericho, and the king thereof, and the mighty men of valour. (Joshua 6:1-2 KJV)

And Joshua rose <u>early</u> in the <u>morning</u>, and the <u>priest</u> took up the <u>ark</u> of the <u>Lord</u>. And <u>seven</u> priest bearing seven <u>trumpets</u> of <u>rams'</u> <u>horns</u> before the ark of the Lord went on continually, and <u>blew</u> with the trumpets: and the <u>armed</u> men went before them; but the rereward came after the ark of the Lord, the priest going on, and blowing with the trumpets.

And the <u>second</u> day they <u>compassed</u> the <u>city</u> once and returned into the <u>camp</u>: so they did <u>six</u> <u>days</u>. And it came to pass on the seventh day, that they rose early about the dawning of the day, and compassed the city after the same manner seven times: only on that day they compassed the city seven times. And it came to pass at the seventh time, when the priests blew with the trumpets, Joshua said unto the people, <u>SHOUT</u>; for the Lord hath <u>given</u> you the city.

And the city shall be <u>accursed</u> even it, and all that are herein, to the Lord: only <u>Rehab</u> the <u>harlot</u> shall live, she and all that are with her in the <u>house</u>, because she <u>hid</u> the <u>messengers</u> that we sent....the <u>wall</u> <u>fell</u> <u>down</u> <u>flat</u>, so that the <u>people</u> went up into the city, every man straight before him, and they <u>took</u> the city. (Joshua 6:12-17, 20 KJV)

GIL Publications, P. O. Box 80275, Brooklyn, NY 11208
www.BibleWordSearchPuzzles.com

```
F  M  A  G  S  A  O  Z  O  B  T  A  L  F  D
L  C  O  C  G  E  R  G  O  N  T  V  O  O  T
D  A  T  R  C  M  C  M  B  I  H  Z  W  U  Y
R  M  B  O  N  U  E  O  E  U  H  N  O  L  G
K  P  L  N  L  I  R  S  N  D  W  H  R  D  F
R  I  E  U  A  R  N  S  D  S  A  P  D  O
A  X  W  M  J  M  A  G  E  E  E  Y  E  F  H
N  V  S  H  C  Z  H  H  R  D  N  S  T  X  K
E  G  R  G  T  D  H  E  T  O  S  G  C  I  X
R  R  W  G  B  A  H  E  H  A  T  L  E  J  C
D  C  W  U  N  A  P  C  P  S  S  K  L  R  G
L  L  I  D  B  M  I  M  E  H  Q  E  O  E  S
I  L  V  Z  U  R  O  I  I  U  Z  G  V  O  F
H  A  X  R  E  C  R  P  J  K  N  M  K  E  T
C  W  T  J  M  P  R  B  O  N  S  M  A  R  N
```

26.The Fall of Jericho

ACCURSED	EARLY	RAMS
ARK	FELL	REHAB
ARMED	FLAT	SECOND
BLEW	HAND	SEVEN
CAMP	HARLOT	SHOUT
CHILDREN	JERICHO	TOOK
CITY	MESSENGERS	TRUMPET
COMPASSED	MORNING	WALL
DOWN	PRIEST	

27. Prosperity

The earth is the Lord's, and everything <u>therein</u>, the world, and all who live in it. (Psalm 24:1 NIV)

But thou shall remember the Lord thy God: for it is he that giveth thee power to get <u>wealth</u>, that he may establish his <u>covenant</u> which he sware unto thy fathers, as it is this day. (Deuteronomy 8:18 KJV)

No one can <u>serve</u> two <u>masters</u>…You cannot serve both God and <u>money</u>. (Matthew 6:24 NIV)

Therefore take no thought, saying, What shall we eat? Or, What shall we drink? Or Wherewithal shall we be <u>clothed</u>?… for your heavenly Father knoweth that ye have <u>need</u> of all these things. But <u>seek</u> ye <u>first</u> the <u>kingdom</u> of God, and all his righteousness; and all these <u>things</u> shall be <u>added</u> unto you. (Matthew 6:31, 32-33 KJV)

But my God will <u>supply</u> all your need according to his <u>riches</u> in <u>glory</u> by Christ Jesus. (Philippians 4:19 KJV)

<u>Honor</u> the Lord with your wealth, with the <u>firstfruits</u> of all your crops; then your barns will be filled to <u>overflowing</u>... (Proverb 3:9-10 NIV)

One man gives freely, yet <u>gains</u> even more; another withholds unduly, but comes to <u>poverty</u>. (Proverb 11:24 NIV)

<u>Lazy</u> hands make a man <u>poor</u>, but <u>diligent</u> hands bring wealth. (Proverb 10:4 NIV)

Beloved, I wish above all things that thou mayest <u>prosper</u> and be in <u>health</u>, even as thy soul prospereth. (3 John 2 KJV)

```
S A S S X L Y R O L G P K J T
D E D D A N Y Z A L O I F N B
I Z H Y S E E K F V N I A F I
T F D C A X S L E G R N L D Q
T P G A I N S R D S E F Y C X
N V H N U R T O T V I I L S M
E R N Y I Y M F O L F R P E Z
G O D Z L W R C R S J S P V F
I N R M D U O C M E G T U R O
L O Y B I H W L L A P N S E V
I H B T E E J S F O S S I S Z
D M S A A P O O R R T T O H N
D F L L H U D E E N E H E R T
Z T T Z L E Y E N O M V E R P
H H W C D N I E R E H T O S S
```

27.Prosperity

ADDED	HONOR	PROSPER
CLOTHES	KINGDOM	RICHES
COVENANT	LAZY	SEEK
DILIGENT	MASTERS	SERVE
FIRST	MONEY	SOUL
FRISTFRUITS	NEED	SUPPLY
GAINS	OVERFLOWING	THEREIN
GLORY	POOR	THINGS
HEALTH	POVERTY	WEALTH

28. Pharisees

"Be on your guard against the yeast of the Pharisees, which is hypocrisy." (Luke 12:1 NIV)

"Woe to you, teachers of the law and Pharisees, you hypocrites! You shut the kingdom of heaven in men's faces. You yourselves do not enter, nor will you let those enter who are trying to…

"Woe to you, teachers of the law and Pharisees, you hypocrites! You give a tenth of your spices—mint, dill and cummin. But you have neglected the more important matters of the law—justice, mercy and faithfulness…

"Woe to you, teachers of the law and Pharisees, you hypocrites! You clean the outside of the cup and dish, but inside you are full of greed and self-indulgence. Blind Pharisee! First clean the inside of the cup and dish, and then the outside also will be clean." (Matthew 23:13-14, 23, 25-26 NIV)

"O generation of vipers, how can ye, being evil, speak good things? For out of the abundance of the heart the mouth speaketh." (Matthew 12:34 KJV)

"Why is my language not clear to you? Because you are unable to hear what I say. You belong to your father, the devil, and you want to carry out your father's desire. He was a murderer from the beginning, not holding to the truth, for there is no truth in him… (John 8:43-44 NIV)

"Leave them, they are blind guides. If a blind man leads a blind man, both will fall into a pit." (Matthew 15:14 NIV)

…the Pharisees went out and laid plans to trap him in his words…But Jesus, knowing their evil intent, said, "You hypocrites, why are you trying to trap me…" (Matthew 22:15, 18 NIV)

…the Pharisees and the teachers of the law began to oppose him fiercely and to besiege him with questions, waiting to catch him in something he might say. (Luke 1153-54 NIV)

But the Pharisees went out and plotted how they might kill Jesus. (Matthew 12:14 NIV)

```
I  H  Y  P  O  C  R  I  C  Y  P  J  P  V  P
O  N  S  E  E  S  I  R  A  H  P  S  R  L  W
E  U  T  T  A  N  A  E  L  C  R  E  O  E  N
N  G  T  E  M  T  U  H  S  E  D  T  C  F  A
E  U  E  S  N  T  R  A  P  R  T  I  A  K  X
G  Y  E  I  I  T  D  I  U  E  T  I  R  E  T
L  L  E  C  S  D  V  M  D  S  T  P  C  G  N
E  E  N  K  N  E  E  L  U  H  W  C  A  A  A
C  C  T  E  U  E  B  J  F  E  D  V  T  U  T
T  R  E  L  B  G  G  U  E  O  H  P  C  G  R
E  E  R  Z  U  X  L  L  B  R  P  S  H  N  O
D  I  D  I  E  N  I  L  U  L  I  P  J  A  P
H  F  D  R  E  H  T  I  D  D  I  S  O  L  M
Y  E  A  S  T  J  J  K  H  T  N  N  E  S  I
S  U  S  Q  U  E  S  T  I  O  N  I  D  D  E
```

28.Pharisees

BESIEGE	HYPOCRICY	OPPOSE
BLIND	IMPORTANT	OUTSIDE
CATCH	INDULGENCE	PHARISEES
CLEAN	INTENT	PLOTTED
DESIRE	JUSTICE	QUESTION
ENTER	KILL	SHUT
FAITHFULNESS	LANGUAGE	TRAP
FIERCELY	MURDER	VIPERS
GUIDES	NEGLECTED	YEAST

29. Tongue

Death and life are in the power of the tongue... (Proverb 18:21 KJV)

Behold, we put bits in the <u>horses</u>' mouths, that they may obey us; and we turn about their whole <u>body</u>. Behold also the <u>ships</u>, which though they be so great, and are driven of fierce winds, yet are they turned about with a very small <u>helm</u>...Even so the <u>tongue</u> is a <u>little member</u>...

Out of the same <u>mouth</u> proceedeth blessing and <u>cursing</u>. My brethren, these things ought not so to be. Doth a <u>fountain</u> send forth at the same place <u>sweet</u> water and <u>bitter</u>? (James 3:3-5, 10-11 KJV)

The tongue of the <u>wise</u> commends knowledge, but the mouth of a <u>fool</u> <u>gushes</u> <u>folly</u>...The tongue that brings healing is a tree of life, but a deceitful tongue <u>crushes</u> the spirit. (Proverb 15:2, 4 NIV)

When words are many, sin is not <u>absent</u>, but he who holds his tongue is wise.

The tongue of the righteous is <u>choice</u> <u>silver</u>, but the heart of the wicked is of little <u>value</u>. (Proverbs 10:19-20 NIV)

A <u>fortune</u> made by a lying tongue is a <u>fleeting</u> <u>vapor</u> and a deadly <u>snare</u>. (Proverb 21:6 NIV)

As a north wind brings <u>rain</u>, so a <u>sly</u> tongue brings <u>angry looks</u>. (Proverb 25:23 NIV)

...he whose tongue is <u>deceitful</u> falls into <u>trouble</u>. (Proverb 17:20 NIV)

...the tongue of the wise is health. (Proverb 12:18 KJV)

...every tongue should confess that Jesus Christ is Lord, to the glory of God the Father. (Philippians 2:11 KJV)

```
G B L F O U N T A I N B Y S T
J N I I V A L U E F T L E N F
L D I T T I N I A R L H E O R
F O F S T T H H Z O S S R E S
Y M O L R E L I F U B T B E W
N R G K E U R E R A U M V F E
S H I P S E C C D N E X C U E
E L Q R C T T E E M M L E H T
R O R E O H C I T S A N G R Y
A O E N O E E S N R E Y X N O
N F G R I C M L I G O H H X L
S U S T I O W Y W L X U S I E
E E F O U Z I V X H V P B U G
S U H T S E S S A A W E S L G
L C H V R N E V A P O R R V E
```

29. Tongue

ABSENT	FORTUNE	SHIPS
ANGRY	FOUNTAIN	SILVER
BITTER	GUSHES	SLY
CHOICE	HELM	SNARE
CRUSHES	HORSES	SWEET
CURSING	LITTLE	TONGUE
DECEITFUL	LOOKS	TROUBLE
FLEETING	MEMBER	VALUE
FOLLY	MOUTH	VAPORR
FOOL	RAIN	WISE

30. Seed

A seed produces after it's own kind: (reap what you sow)

Then God said, "Let the land <u>produce</u> vegetation: <u>seed-bearing</u> <u>plants</u> and <u>trees</u> on the land that bear <u>fruit</u> with seed in it, according to their <u>various</u> <u>kinds</u>." And it was so. The land produced <u>vegetation</u>: plants bearing seed according to their kinds and trees bearing fruit with seed in it according to their kinds. (Genesis 1:11-12 NIV)

Remember this: Whoever <u>sows</u> sparingly will also <u>reap</u> <u>sparingly</u>, and whoever sows generously will also reap <u>generously</u>. (2 Corinthians 9:6 NIV)

"Give, and it will be given to you. A good <u>measure</u>, <u>pressed</u> down, <u>shaken</u> <u>together</u> and <u>running</u> over, will be poured into your <u>lap</u>. For with the measure you <u>use</u>, it will be measured to you." (Luke 8:38 NIV)

A season to plant and a season to harvest:

While the <u>earth</u> <u>remaineth</u>, seedtime and <u>harvest</u> ... shall not <u>cease</u> (Genesis 8:22 KJV)

To every thing there is a <u>season</u>, and a time to every <u>purpose</u> under the heaven: A time to be <u>born</u>, and a time to <u>die</u>; a time to <u>plant</u>, and a time to <u>pluck</u> up that which is planted... (Ecclesiastes 3:1-2 KJV)

Whoever <u>watches</u> the <u>wind</u> will not plant; whoever looks at the <u>clouds</u> will not reap. (Ecclesiastes 11:4 NIV)

He that gathereth in <u>summer</u> is a wise son: but he that sleepeth in harvest is a son that causeth <u>shame</u>. (Proverbs 10:5 KJV)

"I tell you, <u>open</u> your <u>eyes</u> and look at the <u>fields</u>! They are <u>ripe</u> for harvest." (John 4:35 NIV)

```
T  N  F  E  O  P  E  N  R  Q  U  P  R  D  B
E  I  O  T  Y  V  O  P  G  Z  L  E  E  E  N
H  R  U  S  E  E  D  Q  P  U  M  S  A  O  L
A  G  U  R  A  B  S  V  C  M  S  R  I  R  Z
R  W  E  S  F  E  W  K  U  E  I  T  U  L  B
V  I  N  N  A  E  S  S  R  N  A  E  Y  S  Q
E  N  D  P  E  E  C  P  G  T  J  I  H  E  Y
S  D  G  A  S  R  M  U  E  S  O  W  S  H  L
T  Z  R  L  S  S  O  G  D  P  S  B  L  C  G
K  H  E  D  D  N  E  U  S  O  L  L  U  T  N
R  E  N  L  E  V  P  S  S  D  R  A  D  A  I
P  I  E  K  M  O  I  E  H  L  U  P  N  W  R
K  I  A  Z  A  E  R  A  U  D  Y  O  W  T  A
F  H  M  I  H  S  U  O  I  R  A  V  L  J  P
S  B  P  G  S  Q  G  N  I  N  N  U  R  C  S
```

30.Seed

BEARING	OPEN	SHAME
CLOUDS	PLANT	SLEEP
EYES	PLUCK	SOWS
FIELDS	PRESSED	SPARINGLY
FRUIT	PRODUCE	SUMMER
GENEROUSLY	RIPE	USE
HARVEST	RUNNING	VARIOUS
KINDS	SEASON	VEGETATION
LAP	SEED	WATCHES
MEASURE	SHAKEN	WIND

31. The Love of Money

He that loveth <u>silver</u> shall <u>not</u> be <u>satisfied</u> with silver; not he that loveth abundance with increase: this is also <u>vanity</u>. When <u>goods</u> increase, they are increased that eat them: and what good is there to the <u>owners</u> thereof, saving the beholding of them with their <u>eyes</u>? (Ecclesiastes 5:10-11 KJV)

He who loves money shall never have enough. The <u>foolishness</u> of <u>thinking</u> that wealth brings <u>happiness</u>! The more you have, the more you spend, right up to the <u>limits</u> of your <u>income</u>, so what is the advantage of wealth—except perhaps to <u>watch</u> it as it <u>runs</u> through your <u>fingers</u>! (Ecclesiastes 5:10-11 TLB)

"No one can serve <u>two</u> <u>masters</u>. <u>Either</u> he will hate the one and love the other, or he will be <u>devoted</u> to the one and <u>despise</u> the other. You cannot serve both God and <u>Money</u>. (Matthew 6:24 NIV)

For the love of money is the <u>root</u> of all evil: which while some <u>coveted</u> after, they have erred from the faith, and <u>pierced</u> themselves through with many <u>sorrows</u>. (1 Timothy 6:10 KJV)

Keep yourself from the love of money and be content with what you have, because God has said,
    "<u>Never</u> will I leave you;
    never will I <u>forsake</u> you." (Hebrews 13:5 NIV)

```
R  E  S  O  J  N  K  X  V  L  P  C  W  G  S
I  I  T  U  F  O  H  A  I  D  O  O  N  R  K
H  T  U  O  T  T  N  M  E  V  S  I  E  H  L
S  H  Z  Z  H  I  I  V  E  S  K  T  T  M  I
S  E  D  H  T  T  O  T  E  N  S  R  R  O  Q
E  R  S  Y  S  T  E  N  I  A  B  R  N  N  W
N  B  N  A  E  D  H  H  M  O  G  E  Y  E  S
I  Q  N  D  T  S  T  F  D  E  W  O  D  Y  B
P  C  Y  T  I  I  F  D  O  E  M  N  O  B  Y
P  K  G  L  W  A  S  I  E  R  C  O  E  D  M
A  M  O  A  E  O  S  F  N  S  S  R  C  R  S
H  O  T  V  K  O  N  S  I  G  P  A  E  N  S
F  C  L  W  M  T  U  I  Z  E  E  I  K  I  I
H  I  N  E  V  E  R  M  C  U  D  R  S  E  P
S  S  O  R  R  O  W  S  G  A  C  V  S  E  Q
```

31.The Love of Money

COVETED	HAPPINESS	ROOT
DESPISE	INCOME	RUNS
DEVOTED	LIMITS	SATISFIED
EITHER	MASTERS	SILVER
EYES	MONEY	SORROWS
FINGERS	NEVER	THINKING
FOOLISHNESS	NOT	TWO
FORSAKE	OWNERS	VANITY
GOODS	PIERCED	WATCH

32. Forgiveness

If we confess our sins, he is faithful and just and will forgive us our sins and <u>purify</u> us from all unrighteousness. (1 John 1:9 NIV)

"You have heard that it was said, "Eye for eye, and tooth for <u>tooth</u>: But I tell you, do not resist an evil person. If someone <u>strikes</u> you on the right <u>cheek</u>, turn to him the other also...

"You have heard that it was said, "Love your <u>neighbor</u>, and hate your enemy. But I tell you: Love your <u>enemies</u>, and pray for those that <u>persecute</u> you, that you may be sons of your Father in heaven...And if you greet only your brothers, what are you doing more than others?" (Matthew 5:38-39, 43-45a, 47a NIV)

"For if you forgive men when they sin against you, your heavenly Father will also forgive you. But if you do not forgive men their sins, your Father will not forgive your sins. (Matthew 6:14-15 NIV)

See than none <u>render</u> evil for evil unto any man; but ever <u>follow</u> that which is good, both among yourselves and to all men. (1 Thessalonians 5:15 KJV)

<u>Forbearing</u> one another, and forgiving one another, if any man have a <u>quarrel</u> against any, even as Christ <u>forgave</u> you, so also do ye. (Colossians 3:13 KJV)

Do not say, "I'll pay you back for this <u>wrong</u>! <u>Wait</u> for the Lord, and he will deliver you. (Proverb 20:22 NIV)

Then came Peter to him, and said, Lord, how oft shall my brother sin against me, and I forgive him? till seven times?

Jesus saith unto him, "I say not unto thee, <u>Until</u> seven times, but, Until seventy times seven. (Matthew 18:21-22 KJV)

Let all <u>bitterness</u>, and <u>wrath</u>, and anger, and <u>clamour</u>, and evil speaking, be put away from you, with all <u>malice</u>: And be ye kind one to another, <u>tenderhearted</u>, forgiving one another, even as God for Christ's sake hath forgiven you. (Ephesians 4:31-32 KJV)

The <u>discretion</u> of a man <u>deferreth</u> his anger: and it is his glory to pass over a <u>transgression</u>. (Proverb 19:11 KJV)

When they <u>hurled</u> their <u>insults</u> at him, he did not retaliate; when he suffered, he made no <u>threats</u>. Instead, he <u>entrusted</u> himself to him who <u>judges</u> justly. (1 Peter 2:23 NIV)

Then said Jesus, "Father, forgive them; for they know not what they do." (Luke 23:34 KJV)

```
E W C F O R B E A R I N G M T
S N T H L E R R A U Q H A E H
O T E R E L I T N U T L N U D
N E L M A E H O L A I D R E E
O N S U I N K C R C E L F T T
I T T U S E S W E R E E R H U
T R R T N N S G H D R M L R C
E U I I W Y I E R F O J U E E
R S K A J R A R O E T W N A S
C T E W E R U R P J S O X T R
S E S D T O G U K U U S O S E
I D N E M A E K U K R D I T P
D E D A V A G N O R W I G O H
R B L E N E I G H B O R F E N
P C B I T T E R N E S S K Y S
```

32.Forgiveness

BITTERNESS	HURLED	STRIKES
CHEEK	INSULTS	TENDERHEARTED
CLAMOUR	JUDGES	THREATS
DEFER	MALICE	TOOTH
DISCRETION	NEIGHBOR	TRANSGRESSION
ENEMIES	PERSECUTE	UNTIL
ENTRUSTED	PURIFY	WAIT
FORBEARING	QUARREL	WRATH
FORGAVE	RENDER	WRONG

GIL Publications, P. O. Box 80275, Brooklyn, NY 11208
www.BibleWordSearchPuzzles.com

33. Blindness

Having the understanding darkened, being alienated from the life of God through the ignorance that is in them, because of the blindness of their heart: (Ephesians 4:18 KJV)

But if our gospel be hid, it is hid to them that are lost. In whom the god of this world hath blinded the minds of them which believe not, lest the light of the glorious gospel of Christ, who is the image of God should shine unto them. (2 Corinthians 4:3-4 KJV)

"Can the blind lead the blind? Shall they not both fall into the ditch?" (Luke 6:39 KJV)

"...The man who walks in the dark does not know where he is going." (John 12:35 NIV)

Speak to each other about these things every day while there is still time, so that none of you will become hardened against God, being blinded by the glamour of sin. (Hebrews 3:13 TLB)

And I will bring the blind by a way that they know not; I will lead them in paths that they have not known: I will make darkness light before them, and crooked things straight. These things will I do unto them, and not forsake them. (Isaiah 42:16 KJV)

Then spake Jesus again unto them, saying, "I am the light of the world: he that followeth me shall not walk in darkness, but shall have the light of life." (John 8:12 KJV)

"The Spirit of the Lord is upon me, because he hath anointed me to preach the gospel to the poor, he hath sent me to heal the brokenhearted, to preach deliverance to the captives, and recovering sight to the blind, to set at liberty them that are bruised. To Preach the acceptable year of the Lord." (Luke 4:18-19 KJV)

[I pray that] the eyes of your understanding being enlightened: that you may know what is the hope of his calling, and what the riches of the glory of his inheritance in the saints, And what is the exceeding greatness of his power to us-ward who believe, according to the working of his mighty power, which he wrought in Christ when he raised him from the dead, and set him at his own right hand in the heavenly places. (Ephesians 1:18-20 KJV)

```
B H S U O I R O L G T H D G D
S E E D M M O H W H C E N E R
D H C A U C F O E T K I N E E
B E I O R A Q I I O D E L C C
L B N N M T R D O N K E E N O
I Q A E E E T R A R G Y A A V
N D Y J T H C T A Q T R D R E
D R A H G H S D H I D J B O R
F G G U E R G C R D S D I N I
B A O G E P R I A U E K S G N
S R A D L A E F L L O E L I G
W M N A L K A O P N L M C A W
I U C W X Y T W H B E I A X W
A E A L I E N A T E D D N L E
S T E C N A T I R E H N I G G
```

Copyright ☐ GIL PUBLICATIONS 2004

33.Blindness

ALIENATED	GLAMOUR	LEAD
BECOME	GLORIOUS	PLACES
BLIND	GREAT	RECOVERING
CALLING	HARD	SHINE
CROOKED	HEART	THEIR
DARKENED	HID	UNDERSTANDING
DITCH	IGNORANCE	WALKS
ENLIGHTENED	IMAGE	WHOM
EXCEED	INHERITANCE	WROUGHT

34. Solomon's Wisdom

In Gibeon the Lord appeared to Solomon in a dream by night: and God said, Ask what I shall give thee.

Behold, I have done according to thy words: lo, I have given thee a wise and understanding heart; so that there was none like thee before thee, neither after thee shall any arise like unto thee. And I have also given thee that which thou hast not asked, both riches, and honor: so that there shall not be any among the kings like unto thee all thy days. (1 Kings 3:5, 12-13 KJV)

And God gave Solomon wisdom and understanding exceeding much, and largeness of heart, even as the sand that is on the see shore. And Solomon's wisdom excelled the wisdom of all the children of the east country, and all the wisdom of Egypt. For he was wiser than all men: than Ethan the Ezrahite, and Herman, and Chalcol, and Darda, the sons of Mahol: and his fame was in all nations round about.

And he spake three thousand proverbs: and his songs were a thousand and five. And he spake of trees, from the cedar tree that is in Lebanon even unto the hyssop the springeth out of the wall: he spake also of beasts, and of fishes. And there came of all people to hear wisdom of Solomon, from all kings of the earth, which had heard of his wisdom.

Now two prostitutes came to the king and stood before him. One of them said, "My lord, this woman and I live in the same house. I had a baby while she was there with me. The third day after my child was born, this woman also had a baby…

During the night this woman's son died because she lay on him. she … took my son from my side … put him by her breast and her dead son by my breast…The other woman said, "No! The living one is my son; the dead one is yours"

Then the king said, "…Cut the living child in two and give half to one and half to the other."

The woman whose son was alive was filled with compassion… "Please, my lord, give her the living baby! Don't kill him!"

But the other said, "Neither I nor you shall have him. Cut him in two."

Then the king gave his ruling: " Give the living baby to the first woman. Do not kill him; she is his mother."

…Israel …held the king in awe, because they saw he had wisdom from God to administer justice. (1 King 3:16-19, 20, 22, 24, 25-27 NIV)

```
T R T E F R L R B W I G N S R
H J U U G A E A S G N O S V W
O U Z L O Y R T G N I V I L O
U S W G I B P T S S I D R E M
S T N R O N A T S I A T O E A
A I O E U G G A P B N H D V N
N C M Y N T P R H S E I W I B
D E O S A M O D I Y E A M F Y
W A L L O V P I E S S H S D B
D X O C E T N Y P A Y S S T A
H F S R S O Q R T W L D O I S
D Y B A E F I H I E L T T P F
M S E B I N G S A N D L I H C
E R I E G I E B A B Y G M H F
B G Z R N R W Q S N O I T A N
```

34. Solomon's Wisdom

ABOUT	FISHES	RULING
ADMINISTER	FIVE	SAND
AWE	GIBEON	SOLOMON
BABY	HYSSOP	SONGS
BEASTS	JUSTICE	SPRING
BREAST	LIVING	THOUSAND
CHILD	NATIONS	WALL
COMPASSION	NIGHT	WISER
EGYPT	PROVERBS	WOMAN

35. Praise Ye The Lord

I will bless the Lord at <u>all</u> <u>times</u>: his praise shall <u>continually</u> be in my mouth. (Psalm 34:1 KJV)

Praise ye the Lord,
Praise God in his <u>sanctuary</u>:
Praise him in the <u>firmament</u> of his <u>power</u>;
Praise him for his mighty <u>acts</u>;
Praise him according to his <u>excellent</u> greatness.
Praise him with the sound of the <u>trumpet</u>;
Praise him with the <u>psaltery</u> and <u>harp</u>,
Praise him with <u>timbrel</u> and <u>dance</u>:
Praise him with the <u>stringed</u> <u>instruments</u> and <u>organs</u>.
Praise him upon the <u>high</u> <u>sounding</u> <u>cymbals</u>.
Let every thing that hath <u>breath</u> praise the Lord.
Praise ye the Lord. (Psalm 150 KJV)

From the <u>lips</u> of children and infants you have <u>ordained</u> <u>praise</u>, because of your enemies, to <u>silence</u> the foe and the avenger. (Psalm 8:2 NIV)

I call to the Lord, who is <u>worthy</u> of praise, and I am saved from my enemies. (Psalm 18:3 NIV)

What time I am <u>afraid</u>, I will <u>trust</u> in thee. In God I will praise his word, in God I have put my trust; I will not fear what flesh can do unto me. (Psalm 56:3-4 KJV)

```
T A S T S O U N D I N G V C H
P I F T R H I G H U Q J O T E
E O M R N U D A N C E N A S T
X X W B A E S U L P T E I L P
C Y S E R I M T P I R A P Z S
E R U Y R E D U N B R F B X A
L A A N A L L U R P U G N X L
L U S T C A A O C T H A R P T
E T S P I L R S T Y S S E N E
N C N B L D I E W O M N G U R
T N H Y A L P R G O R B I T Y
B A K I E M P T I J R G A H F
K S N N U S A S E M I T A L B
N E C R S T R I N G E D H N S
D E T F I R M A M E N T T Y S
```

35. Praise Ye The Lord

ACTS	HARP	SANCTUARY
AFRAID	HIGH	SILENCE
ALL	INSTRUMENTS	SOUNDING
BREATH	LIPS	STRINGED
CONTINUALLY	ORDAINED	TIMBREL
CYMBALS	ORGANS	TIMES
DANCE	POWER	TRUMPET
EXCELLENT	PRAISE	TRUST
FIRMAMENT	PSALTERY	WORTHY

36. Sins of the Flesh

Works of the Flesh
(Galatians 5:19-21 KJV)

adultery
fornication
uncleanness
lasciviousness
idolatry
witchcraft
hatred
variance
emulation
wrath
strife
sedition
heresies
envying
murders
drunkenness
reveling
and such like

Sinful Nature
(Galatians 5:19-21 NIV)

sexual immorality
impurity
debauchery
idolatry
fits of rage
selfish ambition
dissension
factions
envy
drunkenness
orgies
and the like

```
A  D  U  L  T  E  R  Y  E  A  V  J  N  E  K
I  M  P  U  R  I  T  Y  F  H  X  O  M  C  Q
H  S  I  F  L  E  S  L  E  L  I  U  W  M  M
L  S  U  C  H  U  E  R  A  T  L  G  I  I  N
I  L  I  K  E  V  E  U  A  A  V  S  T  I  F
D  D  T  K  E  S  X  C  T  C  A  P  C  Y  N
U  E  O  R  Y  E  I  I  Y  P  R  S  H  T  O
N  I  B  L  S  N  O  G  V  Q  I  N  C  I  I
C  Z  X  A  R  N  W  Z  N  F  A  O  R  L  S
L  S  Z  O  U  D  S  R  E  C  N  I  A  A  N
E  P  F  O  Y  C  E  T  A  G  C  T  F  R  E
A  Z  R  A  G  E  H  R  R  T  E  C  T  O  S
N  G  P  V  H  F  V  E  T  I  H  A  X  M  S
Y  D  R  U  N  K  E  N  R  A  F  F  E  M  I
S  E  D  I  T  I  O  N  S  Y  H  E  M  I  D
```

36.Sins of the Flesh

ADULTERY	HATRED	SEDITION
DEBAUCHERY	HERESY	SELFISH
DISSENSION	IDOL	SEXUAL
DRUNKEN	IMMORALITY	STRIFE
EMULATION	IMPURITY	SUCH
ENVY	LIKE	UNCLEAN
FACTIONS	ORGY	VARIANCE
FITS	RAGE	WITCHCRAFT
FORNICATION	REVEL	WRATH

37. Patience and Perseverance

...let us <u>lay aside</u> every <u>weight,</u> and the sin which doth so easily <u>beset</u> us, and let us run with patience the <u>race</u> that is set before us, looking unto Jesus the author and <u>finisher</u> of our faith; who for the joy that was set before him <u>endured</u> the cross... (Hebrews 12:1-2 KJV)

...the race is not to the <u>swift,</u> nor the battle to the <u>strong</u>... (Ecclesiastes 9:11 KJV)

Be patient, then brothers, until the Lord's coming. See how the farmer waits for the land to yield its <u>valuable</u> crop and how patient he is for the <u>autumn</u> and spring rains. (James 5:7 NIV)

For I reckon that the sufferings of this present time are not worthy to be compared with the glory which shall be <u>revealed</u> in us. (Romans 8:18 KJV)

Consider it <u>pure</u> joy, my brothers, whenever you face <u>trials</u> of many kinds, because you know that the <u>testing</u> of your faith develops perseverance. <u>Perseverance</u> must finish its work so that you may be <u>mature</u> and <u>complete,</u> not <u>lacking</u> anything. (James 1:2-4 NIV)

For ye have need of patience, that, after ye have done the will of God, ye might receive the promise. (Hebrews 10:36 KJV)

Let us not become <u>weary</u> in doing good, for at the <u>proper</u> time we will reap a harvest if we do not give up. (Galatians 6:9 NIV)

...<u>rejoice</u> in our <u>sufferings,</u> because we know that suffering produces perseverance; perseverance, character; and <u>character,</u> hope. And <u>hope</u> does not <u>disappoint</u> us, because God has <u>poured</u> out his love into our hearts by the Holy Spirit, whom he has given us. (Romans 5:3-5 NIV)

```
P O U R E D C R L A B P L W W
E C I O J E R H E A U E U A N
R V V G I K E I A H C T S R Y
S D E L A E V E R R S K U E E
E R N P R O P E R C A I I M T
V B D E T E L P M O C C N N N
E Y U D I S A P P O I N T I G
R G R S W I F T W E A R Y E F
A T E S T I N G S T A E R G R
N O D O O F E T W H R X Y B V
C E C A R R E B X O A X T M
E C A M U O I F M A E P I H C
U D I T N G P E D I S A E L U
A F A G H V A L U A B L E Q S
W M A T S S G N I R E F F U S
```

37.Patience and Perseverance

ASIDE
AUTUMN
BESET
CHARACTER
COMPLETE
DISAPPOINT
ENDURED
FINISHER
HOPE

LACKING
LAY
MATURE
PERSEVERANCE
POURED
PROPER
PURE
RACE
REJOICE

REVEALED
STRONG
SUFFERINGS
SWIFT
TESTING
TRAILS
VALUABLE
WEARY
WEIGHT

38. Renew Your Mind

And be not <u>conform</u>ed to this world: but be <u>transform</u>ed by the <u>renew</u>ing of your <u>mind</u>, that ye may <u>prove</u> what is that good , and acceptable, and <u>perfect</u>, will of God. (Roman 12:2 KJV)

Do not conform any <u>longer</u> to the <u>pattern</u> of this world, but be transformed by the renewing of your mind. Then you will be able to test and approve what God's will is – his good, pleasing and perfect will. (Romans 12:2 NIV)

Don't <u>copy</u> the behavior and <u>customs</u> of this world, but be a <u>new</u> and <u>different</u> person with a <u>fresh</u> newness in all you do and <u>think</u>. Then you will learn from your own <u>experience</u> how his ways will <u>really</u> <u>satisfy</u> you. (Romans 12:2 TLB)

…put on the new self, which is being renewed in knowledge in the image of its <u>Creator</u>. (Coossians 3:10 NIV)

For it is God which worketh in you both to will and to do his good <u>pleasure</u>. (Philippians 2:13 KJV)

Rather, clothe yourselves with the Lord Jesus Christ, and do not think about how to <u>gratify</u> the desires of the sinful <u>nature</u>. (Roman 13:14 NIV)

For the weapons of our warfare are not <u>carnal</u>, but mighty through God to the pulling <u>down</u> of <u>strongholds</u>; Casting down <u>imaginations</u>, and every high thing that <u>exalteth</u> itself against the knowledge of God, and bringing into <u>captivity</u> every thought to the obedience of Christ. (2 Corinthians 10:4-5 KJV)

```
X  C  E  P  L  E  A  S  U  R  E  O  Y  L  C
N  P  R  X  L  A  W  W  O  U  O  L  A  O  E
D  R  Q  E  A  R  U  E  Y  Q  L  N  N  X  M
I  Y  E  N  A  L  U  N  J  A  R  F  P  H  R
F  Y  P  T  O  T  T  E  E  A  O  E  K  N  O
F  F  I  T  T  I  O  R  C  R  R  P  P  A  F
E  S  N  E  W  A  T  R  M  I  C  O  P  Y  S
R  I  E  V  O  R  P  A  E  K  N  I  H  T  N
E  T  J  S  H  R  Y  N  N  M  T  W  D  D  A
N  A  E  S  E  F  C  W  E  I  O  L  P  E  R
T  S  E  G  I  E  U  O  M  R  G  T  T  A  T
A  R  N  T  M  I  N  D  W  W  U  A  S  R  M
F  O  R  P  T  C  E  F  R  E  P  T  M  U  P
L  A  C  A  P  T  I  V  I  T  Y  S  A  I  C
G  S  T  R  O  N  G  H  O  L  D  U  E  N  B
```

38.Renew Your Mind

CAPTIVITY	EXPERIENCE	PERFECT
CARNAL	FRESH	PLEASURE
CONFORM	GARTIFY	PROVE
COPY	IMAGINATION	REALLY
CREATOR	LONGER	RENEW
CUSTOM	MIND	SATISFY
DIFFERENT	NATURE	STRONGHOLD
DOWN	NEW	THINK
EXALT	PATTERN	TRANSFORM

39. The Word of God

In the beginning was the Word, and the Word was with God, and the Word was God...And the Word was made flesh, and dwelt among us... (John 1:1, 14 KJV)

So shall my word be that goeth forth out of my mouth: it shall not return unto me void, but it shall accomplish that which I please, and it shall prosper in the thing whereto I sent it. (Isaiah 55:11 KJV)

Sanctify them through thy word: thy word is truth. (John 17:17 KJV)

Is not my word like a fire? Saith the Lord; and like a hammer that breaketh the rock in pieces? (Jeremiah (23:29 KJV)

Thy word is a lamp unto my feet, and a light unto my path. (Psalm 119:105 KJV)

So then faith cometh by hearing, and hearing by the word of God. (Roman 10:17 KJV)

For the word of God is quick, and powerful, and sharper than any two-edged sword, piercing even to the dividing of soul and spirit, and of the joints and marrow, and is a discerner of the thoughts and intents of the heart. (Hebrews 4:12 KJV)

...the sword of the spirit, which is the word of God... (Ephesisans 6:17 KJV)

[Jesus] told them, "The secret of the kingdom of God has been given to you...Don't you understand this parable? How then will you understand any parable? The farmer sows the word..." (Mark 4:11, 13-14 NIV)

"The words I have spoken to you are spirit and they are life." (John 6:63 NIV)

```
K K O K Q G N R G G K D T S D
B S L U N W E N N I H R T A I
P T I O O M I I N N U Z W N S
V C M R M N R G R T G N O C C
K A R A N A D U H W B I E T E
A A H I E O T S F Z N K D I R
M C G H M E R D W E S T G F N
Q E C Q R J R S W O E S E Y E
B R B O S E O X K E R T D Z R
C M A H M T L I S E L D T K J
W D R O W P N B N E H T I W X
R F Y E H T L E A T C E C I N
R R B T N E S I T R S E L W E
A A N E K O P S S N A L I B I
S R O C K E R I F H I P O P O
```

39.The Word of God

ACCOMPLISH	INTENTS	SANCTIFY
AMONG	JOINTS	SENT
BEGINNING	KINGDOM	SPOKEN
DISCERNER	MARROW	SWORD
DWELT	PARABLE	THEY
FEET	PIECES	TRUTH
FIRE	QUICK	TWOEDGED
HAMMER	RETURN	WITH
HEARING	ROCK	WORD

40. The Battle is the Lord's

Worship the Lord your God, and his blessing will be on your food and water. I will take away sickness from among you, and I will none will miscarry or be barren in your land. I will give you a full life span.

I will send terror ahead of you and throw into confusion every nation you encounter. I will make all your enemies turn their backs and run. I will send the hornet ahead of you and drive the Hivites, Canaanites and Hittites out of your way.

Little by little I will drive them out before you, until you have increased enough to take possession of the land. (Exodus 23:25-28, 30 NIV)

[T]he children of Moab, and the children of Ammon...came against Jehoshaphat to battle...Jehoshaphat feared, and set himself to seek the Lord, and proclaimed a fast throughout all Judah. And Judah gathered themselves together, to ask help of the Lord even out of all the cities of Judah they came to seek the Lord.

Thus saith the Lord...Be not afraid nor dismayed by reason of this great multitude; for the battle is not yours, but God's...Ye shall not need to fight in this battle: set yourselves, stand ye still, and see the salvation of the Lord with you, O Judah and Jerusalem: fear not ...

And when they began to sing and to praise, the Lord set ambushments against the children of Ammon, Moab, and mount Seir which were come against Judah; and they were smitten.

Thou preparest a table in the presence of mine enemies: thou annointest my head with oil; my cup runneth over. Surely goodness and mercy shall follow me all the days of my life: and I will dwell in the house of the Lord for ever. (Psalm 23:5-6 KJV)

You armed me with strength for battle; you made my adversaries bow at my feet. You made my enemies turn their backs in flight and I destroyed my foes. (Psalm 18:39-40 NIV)

But thanks be to God, which giveth us the victory through our Lord Jesus Christ. (1 Corinthians 15:57 KJV)

```
W  S  I  C  K  N  E  S  S  U  T  H  E  B  E
F  K  N  E  T  T  I  M  S  E  O  N  A  N  V
T  J  N  O  S  A  E  R  R  R  O  R  C  D  F
H  H  V  M  C  Y  V  R  N  U  R  O  M  I  I
P  S  G  C  U  A  O  E  G  E  U  N  I  S  C
R  D  U  I  P  R  T  H  N  N  O  W  S  M  H
E  Q  E  B  L  P  Q  E  T  I  P  O  C  A  E
S  T  H  Y  M  F  X  E  S  G  D  R  A  Y  D
E  M  K  H  O  A  R  U  M  E  E  S  R  E  U
N  N  A  P  S  R  F  B  X  V  L  H  R  D  T
C  N  E  V  E  N  T  A  A  Y  B  I  Y  T  I
E  G  Q  V  O  J  L  S  R  T  A  P  I  S  T
Y  T  I  C  L  B  I  E  E  M  T  Q  K  Y  L
J  R  V  I  C  T  O  R  Y  D  E  L  N  M  U
D  T  V  S  S  E  N  D  O  O  G  D  E  N  M
```

40. The Battle is the Lord's

AMBUSH	ENCOUNTER	PRESENCE
ARMED	ENOUGH	REASON
BARREN	EVEN	SICKNESS
BATTLE	FLIGHT	SMITTEN
CONFUSION	GOODNESS	SPAN
CUP	HORNET	TABLE
DESTROYED	MISCARRY	TERROR
DISMAYED	MULTITUDE	VICTORY
DRIVE	OIL	WORSHIP

41. Jesus Feeds the 5000

Jesus crossed to the far <u>shore</u> of the Sea of Galilee (that is, the Sea of <u>Tiberias</u>), and a great crowd of people followed him because they saw the <u>miraculous</u> <u>signs</u> he had <u>performed</u> on the sick. (John 6:1-2 NIV)

When Jesus landed and saw a large crowd, he had <u>compassion</u> on them, because they were like sheep without a <u>shepherd</u>. So he began to teach them many things. (Mark 6:34 NIV)

[Jesus] said to <u>Philip</u>, "Where shall we <u>buy</u> bread for these people to eat?" He asked only to test him, for he <u>already</u> had in mind what he was going to do. Philip answered him, "<u>Eight</u> months <u>wages</u> would not buy enough bread for each one to have a <u>bite</u>!" (John 6:5-7 NIV)

"Here is a boy with five <u>small</u> <u>barley</u> <u>loaves</u> and two small fish, but how far will they go among so many?" (John 6:9 NIV)

[Jesus] said to his disciples, "Have them sit down in <u>groups</u> of about <u>fifty</u> each." The disciples did so and everybody sat down. Taking the five loaves and the two fish and looking up to heaven, he gave thanks and <u>broke</u> them. Then he gave them to his disciples to set before the people. (Luke 9:14-16 NIV)

When they had all had enough to eat, he said to his disciples, "<u>Gather</u> the pieces that are left over. Let nothing be <u>wasted</u>." So they gathered them and filled <u>twelve</u> <u>baskets</u> with the pieces ...

After the people saw the miraculous sign that Jesus did, they began to say, "<u>Surely</u> this is the Prophet who is to come into the world." Jesus, knowing that they intended to come and make him king by <u>force</u>, <u>withdrew</u> again to a mountain by himself. (John 6:12-15 NIV)

```
T E P E R F O R M E D W M S S
Y F K S P H I L I P B U Y I H
F I S O U I I E B C I U E G O
S F M H R O D V O P W A X N R
A T A E F B L M A G I K O S E
I Y L T L J P U S Y R L T U O
R N L I P A A S C T E O I L E
E Y U B S L H G Z A E L U H F
B F S S R E A I P E R K R P P
I D I E P T S Y W R V I S A S
T O A E H E L A T S N L M A B
N D R E V E S H M R C X E A B
Y D R A R T G W A G E S T W V
C V O U E I F O R C E K J V T
A L S D E I T W E R D H T I W
```

41.Jesus Feeds the 5000

ALREADY	FORCE	SHORE
BARLEY	GATHER	SIGNS
BASKETS	GROUPS	SMALL
BITE	LOAVES	SURELY
BROKE	MIRACULOUS	TIBERIAS
BUY	PERFORMED	TWELVE
COMPASSION	PHILIP	WAGES
EIGHT	PHILIPBUY	WASTED
FIFTY	SHEPERD	WITHDREW

42. Creation

In the beginning God created the heaven and the earth. And the earth was without <u>form,</u> and <u>void;</u> and darkness was <u>upon</u> the face of the deep. And the Spirit of God moved upon the face of the waters.

And God said, Let there be light...And God <u>divided</u> the light from darkness...and called the light Day, and the darkness <u>Night.</u> And the <u>evening</u> and the <u>morning</u> were the first day.

And God said, Let there be a firmament in the <u>midst</u> of the waters, and let it divide the waters from the waters...and it was so...

And God called the <u>dry</u> land Earth and the gatherings together of the waters called Seas...

And God said, Let the Earth bring forth <u>grass,</u> the <u>herb</u> yielding seed and the fruit yielding after his kind, whose seed is in <u>itself</u>...

And God said, Let there be lights in the firmament of the heaven to divide the day from the night; and let them be for signs, and for seasons, and for days and years...

And God said, Let the waters bring forth abundantly moving creature that hath life , and fowl that may <u>fly</u> above the earth in the <u>open</u>...

And God created great <u>whales,</u> and every living creature that <u>moveth</u>...

And God blessed them, saying Be fruitful and <u>multiply</u>...

And God said, Let the earth bring forth the living <u>creature</u> <u>after</u> his kind, cattle, and <u>creeping</u> thing, and beast of the earth....

And God said, Let us make man in our <u>image,</u> after our <u>likeness:</u> and let them have <u>dominion</u> over the fish of the sea, and over the fowl of the air, and over every creeping thing that creepeth upon the earth.

So God created man in his own image, in the image of God created he him, <u>male</u> and <u>female</u> created he them.

And God blessed them...

Thus the heavens and the earth were finished, and all the <u>hosts</u> of them. And on the seventh day God <u>ended</u> his work which he had made...(Genesis 1:1-7, 10, 11, 14, 20, 21, 22, 24, 26-27, 2:1-2 KJV)

```
I U D M O V E F L Y J G W R A
T P C I G E Z W T L A R R K X
S O S R V N E D S H B M V K R
E N O S E I I L E T G R J S J
L T P V E A D N A D S I E I E
F D E O J N T E R M N O N H I
D O N I N H E U D O E E H D G
R E Z D V C V K R B M F O N Y
Y K X V H X Z R I E G M I L E
Z S B I M A G E F L I P P V K
I E A H P F J T G N E I E A A
A L T R U E S R I E T N I F F
P A T U L D A O R L I S T O H
S H J A I S N C U N B E R D C
V W M M S P V M G H R M M E A
```

42.Creation

AFTER	FLY	MIDST
CREATURE	FORM	MORNING
CREEPING	GRASS	MOVE
DIVIDED	HERB	MULTIPLY
DOMINION	HOSTS	NIGHT
DRY	IMAGE	OPEN
ENDED	ITSELF	UPON
EVENING	LIKENESS	VOID
FEMALE	MALE	WHALES

43. More than a Conqueror

For God did not give us a spirit of <u>timidity</u>, but a spirit of power, of love and of <u>self</u>-<u>discipline</u>. (2 Timothy 1:7 NIV)

Ye are of God, little <u>children</u>, and have <u>overcome</u> them: because greater is he that is in you, than he that is in the world. (1 John 4:4 KJV)

I can do all things <u>through</u> Christ which strengtheneth me. (Philippians 4:13 KJV)

If God be for us, who can be <u>against</u> us? (Roman 8:31 KJV)

Who shall <u>separate</u> us from the love of Christ? Shall <u>trouble</u> or <u>hardship</u> or <u>persecution</u> or <u>famine</u> or <u>nakedness</u> or <u>danger</u> or sword? As it is <u>written</u>: For your sake we face <u>death</u> all day <u>long</u>; we are <u>considered</u> as sheep to be <u>slaughtered</u>.

No, in all these things we are more than <u>conquerors</u> through him who loved us. For I am <u>convinced</u> that neither death nor life, neither angels nor <u>demons</u>, neither the <u>present</u> nor the future, nor any powers, neither <u>heights</u> nor <u>depth</u>, nor anything else in all <u>creation</u>, will be able to separate us <u>from</u> the love of God that is in Christ Jesus our Lord. (Romans 8:35-39 NIV)

```
D E M O N C R O R E U Q N O C
S A L U G H T E R D E A T H B
C H I L D R E N P R E S E N T
F P C O N S I D E R D E P T H
W A E E D F E C N I V N O C D
G N M R H A R D S H I P Z A D
D H A I S T H R O U G H N I T
N E D K N E F R O M T G S T I
O T T W E E C W P H E C J R M
I A S R P D F U G R I F Y O I
T R N I J O L I T P R R B U D
A A I T P O E T L I Z O O B I
E P A T L H S I V B O V Q L T
R E G E S N N I X L O N G E Y
C S A N O E O V E R C O M E Q
```

43.More than a Conqueror

AGAINST	DEPTH	PERSECUTION
CHILDREN	DISCIPLINE	PRESENT
CONQUEROR	FAMINE	SALUGHTER
CONSIDER	FROM	SELF
CONVINCE	HARDSHIP	SEPARATE
CREATION	HEIGHT	THROUGH
DANGER	LONG	TIMIDITY
DEATH	NAKED	TROUBLE
DEMON	OVERCOME	WRITTEN

44. The Kingdom of God

Once having been asked by the Pharisees when the kingdom of God would come, Jesus replied, "The kingdom of God does not come with your careful observation, nor will people say, "Here it is,' or 'There it is.' Because the kingdom of God is within you." (Luke 17:20-21 NIV)

For the kingdom of God is not a matter of meat and drink, but righteousness, peace and joy in the Holy Ghost. (Romans 14:17 KJV).

"But seek ye first the kingdom of God, and his righteousness; and all these things shall be added unto you." (Matthew 6:33 KJV)

"Verily, I say unto you, Except ye be converted, and become as little children, ye shall not enter into the kingdom of heaven. Whosoever therefore shall humble himself as this little child, the same is the greatest in the kingdom of heaven. (Matthew 18:3-4 KJV)

So is the kingdom of God, as if a man should cast seed into the ground; and should sleep, and rise night and day, and the seed should spring and grow up, he knoweth not how. For the earth bringeth forth fruit of herself; first the blade, then the ear, after that the full corn in the ear. But when the fruit is brought forth, immediately he putteth in the sickle, because the harvest is come.

Whereunto shall we liken the kingdom of God? or with what comparison shall we compare it. It is like a grain of mustard seed, which, when it is sown in the earth, is less than all the seeds that be in the earth: But when it is sown, it groweth up, and becometh greater than all herbs, and shooteth out great branches; so that the fowls of the air may lodge under the shadow of it. (Mark 4:26-32 KJV)

"What shall I compare the kingdom of God to? It is like yeast that a woman took and mixed into a large amount of flour until it worked all through the dough." (Luke 13:20-21 NIV)

…he spake by a parable, "A sower went out to sow his seed: and as he sowed, some fell by the way side…some fell upon a rock…some fell some fell among thorns…and other fell on good ground…the parable is this: the seed is the word of God. (Luke 8: 4, 5, 6, 7, 8, 11 KJV)

"Unto you it is given the mystery of the kingdom of God…Know ye not this parable? And how then will ye know all parables? The Sower soweth the word. (Mark 4:11, 13-14 KJV)

```
R  H  U  M  E  A  T  V  R  K  M  O  A  C  T
I  T  G  P  W  D  V  F  G  H  B  X  O  B  E
S  U  S  U  O  S  E  C  N  S  J  R  Y  J  J
E  N  F  A  O  U  O  T  E  R  N  Z  N  L  M
N  T  A  W  E  D  U  R  R  A  E  E  K  Y  O
V  O  N  O  T  Y  V  S  C  E  M  T  S  O  M
L  I  K  E  N  A  E  U  T  A  V  O  T  I  P
N  J  B  C  T  H  Y  J  V  H  R  N  U  A  R
I  G  V  I  C  R  Y  O  N  N  O  E  O  N  M
W  Y  O  N  E  E  E  Y  S  M  I  R  F  C  T
J  N  A  T  L  L  L  E  R  I  B  H  N  U  O
U  R  S  B  K  I  D  U  T  X  B  N  T  S  L
B  Y  M  C  R  A  O  Y  W  E  A  V  C  I  M
M  U  I  E  L  L  U  F  A  D  G  R  A  E  W
H  S  V  B  F  S  G  R  O  W  Z  O  L  F  K
```

44. The Kingdom of God

AMOUNT	FULL	OBSERVATION
BLADE	GROW	RISE
BRANCHES	HUMBLE	SICKLE
CAREFUL	JOY	SOWN
CONVERTED	LIKEN	THORNS
CORN	MATTER	UNTO
DOUGH	MEAT	VERILY
EAR	MIXED	WITHIN
FLOUR	MYSTERY	YEAST

45. Salvation

"For <u>God</u> so <u>loved</u> the world, that he gave his only begotten Son, that <u>whosoever</u> believeth in him <u>should</u> not <u>perish</u>, but have <u>everlasting</u> life. For God sent not his Son into the world to condemn the world; but that the world through him might be <u>saved</u>." (John 3:16-17 KJV)

I am not <u>ashamed</u> of the gospel of God for the salvation of everyone who believes: first for the <u>Jew</u>, then for the <u>Gentile</u>. (Romans 1:16 NIV)

That if you <u>confess</u> with your mouth, "Jesus is Lord," and believe in your heart that God <u>raised</u> him from the dead, you will be saved. For it is with your heart that you believe and are <u>justified</u>… (Romans 10:9 NIV)

"He that believeth and is <u>baptized</u> shall be saved, but he that believed not shall be <u>damned</u>.
And these signs shall follow them that believe; in my <u>name</u> shall they cast out <u>devils</u>; they shall speak with new <u>tongues</u>; They shall <u>take</u> up <u>serpents</u>; and if they drink any <u>deadly</u> thing, it shall not <u>hurt</u> them; they shall <u>lay</u> hands on the sick, and they shall <u>recover</u>. (Mark 16:16-18 KJV)

"I tell you the <u>truth</u>, no one can see the kingdom of God unless he is <u>born</u> <u>again</u>." John 3:3 NIV)

For by grace are ye saved through faith; and that not of yourselves: it is a <u>gift</u> of God: Not of works, lest any man should boast. (Ephesians 2:8-9 KJV)

```
D  L  T  T  S  E  U  G  N  O  T  J  V  A  V
W  E  O  R  B  R  W  T  I  K  X  D  S  I  D
H  E  A  V  U  H  L  A  Y  Y  E  H  N  E  H
O  S  V  D  E  T  G  J  F  I  A  E  S  J  H
S  D  V  E  L  D  H  D  F  M  L  I  X  F  S
O  K  O  G  R  Y  M  I  E  I  A  I  C  B  T
E  T  F  I  G  L  T  D  T  R  Q  B  Q  D  N
V  Q  B  C  B  S  A  N  R  P  T  A  K  E  E
E  U  G  O  U  D  E  S  S  E  E  D  S  V  P
R  M  R  J  E  G  S  D  T  S  V  R  O  I  R
D  N  W  N  S  N  A  J  L  I  E  O  I  L  E
P  O  M  D  I  C  V  N  H  U  N  F  C  S  S
K  A  Y  A  V  S  E  W  E  J  O  G  N  E  H
D  V  G  G  O  D  D  E  M  A  N  H  T  O  R
X  A  B  A  P  T  I  Z  E  D  C  M  S  Z  C
```

45.Salvation

AGAIN	GENTILE	RAISED
ASHAMED	GIFT	RECOVER
BAPTIZED	GOD	SAVED
BORN	JEW	SERPENTS
CONFESS	JUSTIFIED	SHOULD
DAMNED	LAY	TAKE
DEADLY	LOVED	TONGUES
DEVILS	NAME	TRUTH
EVERLASTING	PERISH	WHOSOEVER

GIL Publications, P. O. Box 80275, Brooklyn, NY 11208
www.BibleWordSearchPuzzles.com

46. In the House

Unless the Lord builds the house,
    its builders labor in vain.
Unless the Lord watches over the city,
    the watchmen stand guard in vain. (Psalm 127:1 NIV)

"I will show you what he is like who comes to me and hears my words and puts them into practice. He is like a man building a house, who dug down deep and laid the foundation on rock. When a flood came, the torrent struck that house but could not shake it, because it was well built.

But the one who hears my words and does not put them into practice is like a man who built a house in the ground without a foundation. The moment the torrent struck that house, it collapsed and its destruction was complete." (Luke 6:47-49 NIV)

"If a house is divided against itself, that house cannot stand." (Mark 3:25 NIV)

"There is no man that hath left house, or brethren, or sisters, or father, or mother, or wife, or children, or lands, for my sake, and the gospel's, But he shall receive an hundredfold now in this time…" (Mark 10:29-30 KJV)

"In my Father's house there are many mansions: if it were not so, I would have told you. I go to prepare a place for you. And if I go and prepare a place for you, I will come again, and receive you unto myself; that where I am there ye may be also." (John 14:2-3 KJV)

```
L  S  M  R  H  Q  D  E  R  D  N  U  H  R  E
C  S  P  O  E  N  V  S  E  F  I  W  O  M  D
B  L  H  D  T  H  O  B  U  Y  I  B  N  E  V
D  K  S  A  R  H  T  I  B  A  A  G  S  X  O
L  A  I  D  K  A  E  A  T  L  Z  T  V  M  D
D  S  S  P  G  E  U  R  F  A  R  D  U  G  E
E  N  T  M  E  Q  R  G  U  U  D  P  E  E  D
S  O  E  A  S  W  L  O  C  N  K  N  K  Q  O
P  I  R  P  U  T  S  T  C  C  L  K  U  N  O
A  S  S  Z  R  F  I  F  U  K  H  E  A  O  L
L  N  F  H  S  O  L  R  R  H  H  O  S  D  F
L  A  I  R  N  E  T  C  Q  S  J  S  U  S  X
O  M  A  A  S  S  T  N  E  R  R  O  T  S  D
C  E  W  T  V  P  N  E  R  H  T  E  R  B  E
H  N  I  B  U  I  L  D  E  R  S  Q  S  N  G
```

46.In the House

BRETHREN	GUARD	PUTS
BUILDERS	HEARS	ROCK
COLLAPSED	HOUSE	SHAKE
DEEP	HUNDRED	SISTERS
DESTRUCTION	ITSELF	STRUCK
DUG	LABOR	TORRENT
FATHER	LAID	UNLESS
FLOOD	MANSIONS	VAIN
FOUNDATION	MOTHER	WIFE

47. God's Purpose for Me

The Lord will <u>fulfill</u> his purpose for me... (Psalm 138:8 NIV)

Before I <u>formed</u> thee in the <u>belly</u> I knew the; and before thou camest <u>forth</u> out of the womb I <u>sanctified</u> thee and I <u>ordained</u> thee a prophet unto nations. (Jeremiah 1:5 KJV)

A man's <u>steps</u> are <u>directed</u> by the Lord. How then can <u>anyone</u> understand his own way? (Proverb 20:24 NIV)

For we are God's <u>workmanship</u>, <u>created</u> in Christ Jesus to do good works, which God prepared in <u>advance</u> for us to do. (Ephesians 2:10 NIV)

For whom he did <u>foreknow,</u> he also did <u>predestinate</u> to be conformed to the image of his Son, that he <u>might</u> be the firstborn among many brethern. Moreover whom he did predestinate, them he also called, them he also <u>justified</u>: and whom he justified, them he also <u>glorified</u>. (Romans 8:29-30 KJV)

Many are the plans in a man's heart, but it is the Lord's purpose that <u>prevails</u>. (Proverb 19:21 NIV)

For it is God which worketh in you both to will and to do his good <u>pleasure</u>. (Philippians 2:13 KJV)

...being <u>confident</u> of this, that he who began a work in you will <u>carry</u> it on to <u>completion</u> until the day of Christ Jesus. (Philippians 1:6 NIV)

For I know the thoughts that I think <u>toward</u> you, saith the Lord, thought of peace, and not of evil, to give you an <u>expected</u> end. Then shall ye call upon me, and ye shall go and pray unto me, and I will <u>hearken</u> unto you. And ye shall seek me, and find me, when ye shall <u>search</u> for me with all your heart. (Jeremaih 29:11-13 KJV)

```
W O R K M A N S H I P E M A C
D E T A N I T S E D E R P D D
E F E E E N O Y N A F H H E E
I U R X V G M J V D W C E R I
F L U P P R E V A I L R A O F
I F S E S T E P S X C A R L I
T I A C H T R O F F R E K P R
S L E T T H G I M L L S E X O
U L L E T O W A R D S E N E L
J I P D Y S D E N I A D R O G
C R E A T E D F O R E K N O W
D E T C E R I D E C N A V D A
T N E D I F N O C D E M R O F
C O M P L E T I O N Y L L E B
Y R R A C D E I F I T C N A S
```

47.God's Purpose for Me

ADVANCE	EXPECTED	ORDAINED
ANYONE	FOREKNOW	PLEASURE
BELLY	FORMED	PREDESTINATE
CAME	FORTH	PREVAIL
CARRY	FULFILL	SANCTIFIED
COMPLETION	GLORIFIED	SEARCH
CONFIDENT	HEARKEN	STEPS
CREATED	JUSTIFIED	TOWARD
DIRECTED	MIGHT	WORKMANSHIP

48. Cleanse Me So I Might Serve Thee

If a man cleanse himself …he will be an instrument for noble purposes, made holy, useful to the Master and prepared to do any good work. (2 Timothy 2:21 NIV)

Have mercy on me, O God…blot out my transgressions. Wash me thoroughly from mine iniquity, and cleanse me from my sin. For I acknowledge my transgressions…Purge me with hyssop, and I shall be clean: wash me, and I shall be whiter than snow.

Create in me a clean heart, O God; and renew a right spirit within me. Cast me not away from thy presence; and take not thy holy spirit from me.

Restore unto me the joy of thy salvation; and uphold me with thy free spirit. Then I will teach transgressors thy ways: and sinners shall be converted unto thee. (Psalm 51:1, 2-3, 7, 10-13 KJV)

```
U P R E T F B B Y A W A R U G
E P E Y I O M T W A F I S S J
C R H W D I I E S P G E R F N
F L O O E B N A S H F E L L D
Z A E T L N E C T U N E T U L
T Z T A S D E H L N S T R L D
T N O N N E A R I M H N W R O
J R L K E S R S I O W A S H Y
J A B U W M E H R O E V A H T
V V S H E R U O H C D V X A I
H G I G E Y U R N Y L O X V U
W T R T C G H S T O S E Z I Q
E U S R H P O N Y S B S A H I
P A E L C N L O E D N L O N N
M M Y V A C Y W O Y T I E P I
```

48.Cleanse Me So I Might Serve Thee

AWAY	INIQUITY	RIGHT
BLOT	INSTRUMENT	SINNERS
CLEAN	MASTER	SNOW
CLEANSE	MERCY	TEACH
FREE	MINE	THOROUGHLY
HAVE	NOBLE	UPHOLD
HIMSELF	PURGE	USEFUL
HOLY	RENEW	WASH
HYSSOP	RESTORE	WHITE

49. The Flood - Noah

The Lord saw how great man's wickedness on the earth had become, and that every <u>inclination</u> of his heart was only evil all the time. The Lord was <u>grieved</u> that he had made man on the earth, and his heart was filled with pain. So the Lord said, I will <u>wipe</u> <u>mankind</u>, whom I have created ... (Genesis 6:5-7 NIV)

But <u>Noah</u> found favor in the eyes of the Lord ... Noah was a righteous man, <u>blameless</u> among the people of this time, and he walked with God. Noah had three sons: <u>Shem</u>, <u>Ham</u> and <u>Japheth</u>. (Genesis 6:8-10 NIV)

Now the earth was corrupt in God's <u>sight</u> and full of <u>violence</u>...So god said to Noah, "I am going to put an end to all people...So make yourself an <u>ark</u> of <u>cypress</u> <u>wood</u>; make rooms in it and coat it with <u>pitch</u> <u>inside</u> and out...I'm going to bring <u>floodwaters</u> on the earth to destroy all life under the heavens...But I am going to establish my covenant with you...You are to bring into the ark two of all living creatures, male and female to keep them alive with you... (Genesis 6:11, 13, 14, 17, 18, 19 NIV)

Noah did everything just as the Lord commanded him...The Lord then said to Noah, "Go into the ark, you and your whole family, because I found you righteous in this <u>generation</u>. Take with you seven of every kind of clean animal...and two of every kind of unclean animal...(Genesis 6:22, 7:1-2 NIV)

Noah was <u>six</u> hundred years old when the floodwaters came on the earth. For forty days and <u>forty</u> nights the flood kept coming on the earth, and as the waters increased they <u>lifted</u> the ark, high above the earth. The waters flooded the earth for a hundred and fifty days. But God remember Noah and all the wild animals and <u>livestock</u> that were with him in the ark and he sent a <u>wild</u> wind over the earth, and the waters <u>receded</u>. (Genesis 7:5, 17, 24, 8:1 NIV)

So Noah came out...then Noah built an alter to the Lord...Then God blessed Noah..."Be <u>fruitful</u> and increase in <u>number</u>, and fill the earth...Never again will the waters become a flood to destroy all life. Whenever the <u>rainbow</u> appears in the clouds, I will see it and remember the everlasting covenant between God and all living creatures..." (Genesis 8:18, 20, 9:15-16 NIV)

```
J  P  V  S  S  E  L  E  M  A  L  B  L  G  L
S  A  I  R  A  I  N  B  O  W  J  A  R  U  U
G  S  P  T  R  S  I  X  A  I  P  I  F  P  D
E  S  E  H  C  B  I  M  R  P  E  T  N  N  V
N  S  R  R  E  H  E  F  K  V  I  O  I  J  I
E  F  S  E  P  T  U  N  E  U  I  K  P  M  O
R  V  C  K  T  Y  H  D  R  T  N  O  A  H  L
A  E  P  I  W  A  C  F  A  A  T  W  D  C  E
T  D  L  I  W  S  W  N  M  S  H  E  M  M  N
I  I  K  L  I  L  I  D  R  E  X  O  A  A  C
O  L  L  G  I  L  Y  Y  O  E  D  N  X  H  E
N  N  H  F  C  T  M  Y  T  O  B  I  E  D  D
G  T  T  N  R  R  W  O  O  D  L  M  S  Q  Q
L  E  I  O  D  E  D  E  C  E  R  F  U  N  U
D  Q  F  K  K  C  O  T  S  E  V  I  L  N  I
```

49.The Flood (Noah)

ARK	INCLINATION	RAINBOW
BLAMELESS	INSIDE	RECEDED
CYPRESS	JAPHETH	SHEM
FLOODWATERS	LIFTED	SIGHT
FORTY	LIVESTOCK	SIX
FRUITFUL	MANKIND	VIOLENCE
GENERATION	NOAH	WILD
GRIEVED	NUMBER	WIPE
HAM	PITCH	WOOD

50. Please God Not Man

Then they called them in again and commanded them not to speak or teach at all in the name of Jesus. But <u>Peter</u> and <u>John</u> replied, "<u>Judge</u> for yourselves <u>whether</u> it is right in God's sight to <u>obey</u> you rather than God. For we cannot help <u>speaking</u> about what we have seen and <u>heard</u>. (Acts 4:18-19 NIV)

And when they had brought them, they set them before the <u>council</u>: and the high priest asked them. Saying, Did not we <u>straitly</u> command you that ye should not teach in this name? and behold, ye have filled Jerusalem with your <u>doctrine</u>, and <u>intend</u> to bring this man's <u>blood</u> upon us. Then Peter and the other <u>apostles</u> answered and said, We ought to obey God <u>rather</u> than men. (Act 5:27-29 KJV)

Yet at the same time many even among the <u>leaders</u> believed in him. But because of the Pharisees they would not confess their faith for <u>fear</u> they would be put out of the <u>synagogue</u>; for they loved praise from men more than praise from God. (John 12:42-43 NIV)

"I do not <u>accept</u> praise from men, but I know you. I know you do not have the love of God in your hearts...How can you believe if you accept praise from one another, yet make no effort to obtain the praise that comes from the only God...If you believed <u>Moses</u>, you would believe Me, for he <u>wrote</u> about me." (John 5:41-42, 44, 46 NIV)

Those controlled by the <u>sinful</u> nature cannot <u>please</u> God. (Romans 8:8 NIV)

And without faith it is <u>impossible</u> to please God, because anyone who comes to him <u>must</u> believe that he <u>exists</u> and that he <u>rewards</u> those who <u>earnestly</u> seek him. (Hebrews 11:6 NIV)

GIL Publications, P. O. Box 80275, Brooklyn, NY 11208
www.BibleWordSearchPuzzles.com

```
S P B K R M E G D U J H I L R
S T L L J S R A E F E M I E E
Y T S E O Q O T Z A P C W S S
N J B I A O E I R O N A I W T
A G M E X S D D S U R A O R R
G N D R R E E S O D R V B O A
O I R I R E I C S P Q S E T I
G K E E L B A A S R Z A Y E T
U A T F L I W R P R E H T T L
E E E E N A S H N O E H S J Y
W P P T C I W B E E S D T D N
U S E C N I M U G T S T A A K
Q N E F N B N H O J H T L E R
D P U M O S E S A W T E L E L
T L N G E N I R T C O D R Y S
```

50.Please God Not Man

ACCEPT	IMPOSSIBLE	PRAISE
APOSTLES	INTEND	RATHER
BLOOD	JOHN	REWARDS
COUNCIL	JUDGE	SINFUL
DOCTRINE	LEADERS	SPEAKING
EARNESTLY	MOSES	STRAITLY
EXISTS	OBEY	SYNAGOGUE
FEAR	PETER	WHETHER
HEARD	PLEASE	WROTE

51. God's Power for Us

...Power <u>belong</u>eth unto God. (Psalm 62:11 KJV)

But we have this <u>treasure</u> in <u>jars</u> of <u>clay</u> to show that this all-<u>surpassing</u> <u>power</u> is from God and not from us. (2 Corinthians 4:7 NIV)

"Do not <u>leave</u> Jerusalem, but wait for the <u>gift</u> my Father <u>promised</u>, which you have heard me speak about...But you will receive power when the Holy Spirit comes on you..." (Acts 1:4,8 NIV)

"Behold, I give <u>unto</u> you power to <u>tread</u> on <u>serpents</u> and <u>scorpions,</u> and over all the power of the enemy: and nothing shall by any means <u>hurt</u> you. (Luke 10:19 KJV)

I pray that out of his <u>glorious</u> <u>riches</u> he may strengthened you with power through his Spirit in your inner <u>being</u>. (Ephesians 3:16 NIV) Now unto him that is able to dso <u>exceeding</u> abundantly above all that we <u>ask</u> or <u>think,</u> according to the power that worketh in us. (Ephesians 3:20 KJV)

He gives <u>strength</u> to the <u>weary</u> and increases the power of the weak. (Isaiah 40:29 NIV)

But he said to me, "My <u>grace</u> is <u>sufficient</u> for you, for my power is <u>made</u> <u>perfect</u> in <u>weakness</u>." (1 Corinthians 12:9 NIV)

```
S T E X C E E D I N G J U A W
I U R I Y E J T R U H N E E P
P J O E E P A F M P T Y A E N
R T P I A C C I A O L R R S L
O R C B R D A G D W Y F V S S
M E S L T O M R E J E G N E T
I A P O U N L J G C N I Y N N
S S L E A V E G T I F N D K E
E U T H I N K I S A P J Z A P
D R H Z G Q R S C G A O Y E R
F E S J G I A E F I N O W W E
V O R N C P S R A J F O V E S
M W I H R Y K C L A Y F L P R
Z E E U H T G N E R T S U E P
B S S P S N O I P R O C S S B
```

51.God's Power for Us

ASK	JARS	STRENGTH
BEING	LEAVE	SUFFICIENT
BELONG	MADE	SURPASSING
CLAY	PERFECT	THINK
EXCEEDING	POWER	TREAD
GIFT	PROMISED	TREASURE
GLORIOUS	RICHES	UNTO
GRACE	SCORPIONS	WEAKNESS
HURT	SERPENTS	WEARY

52. Freedom In Christ

Then <u>Jesus</u> said to those <u>Jews</u> who believed on him, "If ye <u>continue</u> in my word, then are ye my <u>disciples</u> indeed: And ye shall know the truth, and the truth shall make you <u>free</u>...<u>Verily</u>, verily, I say unto you, Whosoever <u>commit</u>teth sin is the servant of sin....If the Son therefore shall make you free, ye shall be free indeed." (John 8:42, 34, 36 KJV)

Now the Lord is the Spirit, and where the <u>Spirit</u> if the Lord is, there is freedom. And we, who with <u>unveiled</u> <u>faces</u> all <u>reflect</u> the Lord's <u>glory</u>, are being <u>transformed</u> into his <u>likeness</u>... (2 Corinthians 3:17-18 NIV)

For you did not receive a spirit that make you a <u>slave</u> <u>again</u> to fear, but you received the spirit of <u>sonship</u>. And by him we <u>cry</u>, "<u>Abba</u>, Father."... (Romans 8:15 NIV)

You have been set free from sin and have become slaves to righteousness...When you were slaves to sin, you were free from the <u>control</u> of righteousness...But now that you have been set free from sin and have become slaves to God, the <u>benefit</u> you reap leads to <u>holiness</u>. (Romans 6:18, 20, 22 NIV)

For the law of the Spirit of life in Christ Jesus hath made me free from the law of sin and death. (Romans 8:2 KJV)

For he that is dead is freed from sin. Now if we be dead with Christ, we believe that we shall also live with him... (Romans 6:7-8 KJV)

<u>Stand</u> <u>fast</u> therefore in the <u>liberty</u> wherewith Christ hath made us free, and be not <u>entangled</u> again with the yoke of <u>bondage</u>. (Galatians 5:1 KJV)

```
B N U M P I H S N O S F J T B
C O A G A I N P U I A E I X L
O I N T B U N I M S S F S O O
N D D D B I T R T U E L R K H
T E S E A H C I S N B T C T S
I L Y B M G B T E S N R R C S
N I M J X R E B E O B A Y E E
U E J E W S O L C V V J F L N
E V V R T Y P F L S E C A F I
J N J A L I C N S I H Z S E L
S U N I C O T D I N B F D R O
L D R S M G L O R Y A E D M H
A E I M S I C E E R F R R O N
V D I L I K E N E S S D T T J
E T S V K S E L G N A T N E Y
```

52.Freedom In Christ

ABBA	ENTANGLES	LIKENESS
AGAIN	FACES	REFLECT
BENEFIT	FAST	SLAVE
BONDAGE	FREE	SONSHIP
COMMIT	GLORY	SPIRIT
CONTINUE	HOLINESS	STAND
CONTROL	JESUS	TRANSFORMED
CRY	JEWS	UNVEILED
DISCIPLES	LIBERTY	VERILY

53. Do Not Worry

"Martha, Martha … you are worried and upset about many things, but only one thing is needed. Mary has chosen what is better and it will not be taken away from her." (Luke 10:41-42 NIV)

"…The one who received the seed among the thorns is the man who hears the word, but the worries of this life and the deceitfulness of wealth choke it, making it unfruitful…" (Matthew 13:22 NIV)

"… You cannot serve both God and money. Therefore I tell you, do not worry about your life, what you will eat and drink, or about your body, what you will wear. Is not life more important than food, and the body more important that clothes? Look at the birds of the air; they do not sow or reap or store away in barns, and yet your heavenly Father feeds them. Are you not much more valuable than they? Who of you by worrying can add a single hour to his life? …Oh you of little faith. So do not worry … your heavenly Father knows that you need them.
But seek first his kingdom and his righteousness, and all these things will be given to you as well." (Matthew 6:24, 25-27, 30, 31, 32-33 NIV)

Let him have all your worries and cares, for he is always thinking about you and watching everything that concerns you. (1 Peter 5:7 TLB)

```
W R X C O S B S D O O F U C W
A A E P H D W T K G L S O N W
T U H T L O I O S W S N U E D
C G A T T U K R I Y C F A H Y
H R Y D R E F E Z E Z L H F B
W P C P W A B T R U T A K E N
E N R D D A M N I H G B O D Y
A W F E E D S E C U N V Y H E
R P J F E E L A A U R E A P H
A Z S U L B T I N B Q F V T T
P U Q T A S K R N N S B N I X
E L T U E N C H O S E N H U G
I I L R I V C O T J G B R Q P
L A A H R V N U P S E T F A D
V C T M M P F R Y R R O W P B
```

53.Do Not Worry

ADD	CONCERNS	THEY
AIR	FEEDS	THINK
BARNS	FOOD	UNFRUITFUL
BETTER	GIVEN	UPSET
BODY	HOUR	VALUABLE
CANNOT	LITTLE	WATCH
CARES	MARTHA	WEALTH
CHOKE	STORE	WEAR
CHOSEN	TAKEN	WORRY

54. Rest for Our Souls

"Come unto me, all ye that <u>labor</u> and are <u>heavy</u> <u>laden</u>, and I will give you <u>rest</u>. Take my <u>yoke</u> upon you, and <u>learn</u> of me; for I am <u>meek</u> and <u>lowly</u> in heart: and ye shall find rest unto your souls. For my yoke is <u>easy</u>, and my burden is <u>light</u>." (Matthew 11:28-30 KJV)

"I have told you all these things, so that in me you will have <u>peace</u>. In this world you will have <u>trouble</u>. But take heart! I have overcome the world." John 16:33 NIV)

Who were they who <u>heard</u> and <u>rebelled</u>? Were they not all those Moses led out of <u>Egypt</u>? ... And to whom did God <u>swear</u> that they would never <u>enter</u> his rest if not to those who <u>disobeyed</u>? So we see that they were not able to enter, because of their own <u>unbelief</u>. (Hebrews 3:16, 18-19 NIV)

Therefore, since the promise of entering his rest still stands, let us be <u>careful</u> that none of you be found to have fallen short of it...the <u>message</u> they heard was of no value to them, because those who heard did not <u>combine</u> it with faith. Now, we who have believed enter his rest... (Hebrews 4:1, 2-3 NIV)

...for anyone who enters God's rest also rests from his own <u>work</u>... (Hebrews 4:10 NIV)

Cast thy <u>burden</u> upon the Lord, and he shall <u>sustain</u> thee: he shall never <u>suffer</u> the righteous to be <u>moved</u>. (Psalm 55:22 KJV)

```
R  C  N  U  E  N  E  C  A  E  P  H  Y  C  E
S  E  Y  E  R  E  S  T  C  H  E  G  A  G  L
G  O  F  Q  D  E  E  L  V  A  E  R  A  E  R
S  Y  D  F  D  A  H  A  R  R  E  S  A  E  A
W  M  S  E  U  K  L  D  D  F  S  R  J  A  K
E  M  H  V  L  S  W  E  U  E  N  H  Z  S  R
A  E  B  A  P  L  Y  L  M  H  E  A  V  Y  O
R  K  R  Q  R  E  E  F  C  T  T  I  Z  A  W
M  O  I  O  B  R  N  B  E  O  Y  L  W  O  L
E  Y  B  O  T  B  Q  I  E  I  M  H  V  P  L
O  A  S  P  U  A  R  U  A  R  L  B  D  R  C
L  I  Y  R  J  L  I  G  H  T  T  E  I  P  Y
D  G  D  M  E  E  K  S  O  S  S  H  B  N  F
E  E  M  O  V  E  D  M  E  Y  E  U  E  N  E
N  T  R  O  U  B  L  E  N  T  E  R  S  M  U
```

54. Rest for Our Souls

BURDEN	LABOR	REBELLED
CAREFUL	LADEN	REST
COMBINE	LEARN	SUFFER
DISOBEYED	LIGHT	SUSTAIN
EASY	LOWLY	SWEAR
EGYPT	MEEK	TROUBLE
ENTER	MESSAGE	UNBELIEF
HEARD	MOVED	WORK
HEAVY	PEACE	YOKE

55. Wisdom Speaks

…fools die for want of <u>wisdom</u>…" (Proverbs 10:21 KJV)

The fear of the Lord is the beginning of wisdom: and the knowledge of the <u>holy</u> is understanding. (Proverbs 9:10 KJV)

For wisdom is better than <u>rubies</u>: and all the things that may be desired are not to be compared to it.

I wisdom dwell with <u>prudence</u>, and find out knowledge of <u>witty</u> inventions.

The fear of the Lord is to hate evil: pride, and <u>arroganc[e]</u>, and the evil way, and the froward mouth, do I hate.

<u>Counsel</u> is mine, and <u>sound</u> wisdom: I am understanding; I have strength.

By me kings <u>reign</u>, and princes <u>decree</u> justice.

By me princes <u>rule</u>, and nobles, even all the <u>judges</u> of the earth.

I love them that love me; and those that seek me <u>early</u> shall find me.

<u>Riches</u> and <u>honor</u> are with me; yea, <u>durable</u> riches and righteousness.

My <u>fruit</u> is better than <u>gold</u>; and my <u>revenue</u> than choice <u>silver</u>. (Proverb 8:11-19 KJV)

The Lord brought me forth as the first of his works, before his deeds of <u>old</u>.

I was appointed from <u>eternity</u>, from the beginning; before the world began.

When there were no <u>oceans</u>, I was given <u>birth</u>…

before the <u>mountains</u> were settled in place, before the <u>hills</u>, I was given birth, before he made the earth or its fields or any of the <u>dust</u> of the worlds.

I was there when he set the heavens in place, when he marked out the <u>horizon</u> on the face of the deep, when he established the <u>clouds</u> above … when he gave the sea its boundary…

I was the <u>craftsman</u> at his side. (Proverbs 8:22-30 NIV)

```
D Z S R P R U D E N C E Y P U
G E O I E Y H O R I Z O N V R
R L C S L I T P Q D L O G U Y
Y F E R N V G T B R H W B L C
P C R C E A E N I G V I R L D
D C E H N E E R P W E A O N U
S Y V O Z A P C X S E U A R R
N T E L E J G F O J D M D U A
I I N Y W X S O U S S U U L B
A N U B N O W D R T B V C E L
T R E U U I G H F R T I V V E
N E C N S E I A M R A I R C V
U T D D S L R M H Z U L U T S
O E O D L C G Y C T S U D R H
M M F S K A R L E S N U O C F
```

55.Wisdom Speaks

ARROGANCE	ETERNITY	PRUDENCE
BIRTH	FRUIT	REIGN
CLOUDS	GOLD	REVENUE
COUNSEL	HILLS	RUBIES
CRAFTSMAN	HOLY	RULE
DECREE	HORIZON	SILVER
DURABLE	JUDGES	SOUND
DUST	MOUNTAINS	WISDOM
EARLY	OCEANS	WITTY

56. Fear Not

The word of the Lord came unto <u>Abram</u> in a vision, saying, <u>Fear</u> not, Abram: I am thy <u>shield</u>, and thy exceeding <u>great</u> reward. (Genesis `15:1 KJV)

And the Lord <u>appeared</u> unto him [<u>Isaac</u>] the <u>same</u> <u>night</u>, and said, I am the God of <u>Abraham</u> thy father: fear not, for I am with thee, and will bless thee, and multiply thy seed for my servant Abraham's sake. (Genesis 26:24 KJV)

And he said, I am God, the God of thy father: fear not to go down into Egypt; for I will there make of thee [<u>Jacob</u>] a great <u>nation</u>:

Moses said unto the people, Fear ye not, stand <u>still</u>, and see the <u>salvation</u> of the Lord, which he will show to you today: for the Egyptians whom ye have seen <u>today</u>, ye shall see them again no more <u>forever</u>. (Exodus 14:13 KJV)

And the Lord said unto <u>Joshua</u>, Fear not, neither be thou <u>dismayed</u>: take all the people of war with thee, and arise, go up to Ai: see, I have given into thy hand the king of Ai, and his people, and his city, and his land.: And thou shall do to Ai and her king as thou didst unto Jericho and her <u>king</u>… (Joshua 8:1-2 KJV)

What time I am <u>afraid</u>, I will <u>trust</u> in thee. In God I will <u>praise</u> his word, in God I have put my trust; I will not fear what <u>flesh</u> can do unto me. (Psalm 56:3-4 KJV)

For he hath said, I will never <u>leave</u> thee, not <u>forsake</u> thee. So that we may <u>boldly</u> say, The Lord is my <u>helper</u>, and I will not fear what man shall do unto me. (Hebrews 13:5-6 KJV)

For God hath not given us the spirit of fear; but of power, and of <u>love</u>, and of a sound <u>mind</u>. (2 Timothy 1:7 KJV)

```
Q  S  N  R  D  K  I  F  I  O  N  F  H  N  Q
I  L  H  O  E  G  F  K  O  S  A  E  X  W  P
U  E  H  I  I  P  V  A  M  R  A  U  R  E  L
M  A  Q  S  E  T  L  D  P  O  S  A  R  M  C
L  V  W  L  E  L  A  E  E  P  D  A  C  A  Z
L  E  G  R  U  L  D  N  H  Y  E  Y  K  S  W
I  L  D  R  A  E  F  Z  S  A  A  A  T  E  D
T  O  Y  G  F  N  I  A  B  H  A  M  R  Z  E
S  V  A  N  S  A  L  R  R  F  J  U  S  E  S
B  E  D  I  X  V  A  E  R  O  E  A  G  I  D
O  F  O  K  A  H  V  A  S  S  B  R  P  F  D
C  S  T  T  A  E  I  H  I  R  E  L  H  L  O
A  D  I  M  R  D  U  A  A  A  D  P  P  N  W
J  O  A  O  T  A  R  M  T  M  I  N  D  L  N
N  C  F  T  R  P  N  I  G  H  T  U  E  O  J
```

56. Fear Not

ABRAHAM	FORSAKE	MIND
ABRAM	GREAT	NATION
AFRAID	HELPER	NIGHT
APPEARED	ISAAC	PRAISE
DISMAYED	JACOB	SALVATION
DOWN	JOSHUA	SAME
FEAR	KING	SHIELD
FLESH	LEAVE	STILL
FOREVER	LOVE	TODAY

57. Jesus Raises Lazarus from the Dead

Now a man named <u>Lazarus</u> was <u>sick</u>. He was from
<u>Bethany</u>, the <u>village</u> of Mary and her sister Martha…When he
heard this, Jesus said, "This sickness will not end in death. No, it
is for God's glory so that God's Son may be <u>glorified</u> through it.
Jesus loved Martha and her <u>sister</u> and Lazarus. Yet when he heard
that Lazarus was sick, he <u>stayed</u> where he was <u>two</u> more days.
Then he said to his disciples, "Let's go to <u>Judea</u>…Our <u>friend</u>
Lazarus has fallen <u>asleep</u>; but I am going there to <u>wake</u> him up."

On his <u>arrival</u>, Jesus found that Lazarus had already been in
the <u>tomb</u> for <u>four</u> days…and many Jews had come to Mary and
Martha to comfort them in the loss of their <u>brother</u>…he was deeply
moved in spirit and troubled. Where have you laid him?" he
asked. Come and see, Lord," they replied.

Jesus <u>wept</u>.

Jesus, once more deeply moved, came to the tomb. It was a
<u>cave</u> with a stone laid across the entrance. "Take away the stone,"
he said. "But Lord," said Martha, the sister of the dead man. "By
this time there is a bad <u>odor</u>, for he has been there for four days."

Then Jesus said, "Did I not tell you that if you believed, you
would see the glory of God?" So they took away the <u>stone</u>. Then
Jesus looked up and said, "Father, I thank you that you have heard
me. I knew that you <u>always</u> hear me, but I said this for the benefit
of the people standing here, that they may believe that you <u>sent</u>
me."

When he had said this, Jesus called in a <u>loud</u> <u>voice</u>,
"Lazarus, come out!" The dead man came out, his hands and feet
<u>wrapped</u> with <u>strips</u> of linen and a cloth around his <u>face</u>. Jesus said
to them, "Take off the <u>grave</u> clothes and let him go." (John 11:1,
4-7, 11, 17, 19, 33-35, 38-44 NIV)

```
S  A  S  X  N  O  G  A  F  N  L  Z  L  F  P
H  Y  C  T  T  Z  R  L  A  E  S  S  A  E  A
M  R  A  Q  O  M  A  O  C  E  U  A  E  E  T
R  L  U  W  E  N  V  U  E  R  G  L  D  Z  O
Z  F  S  O  L  C  E  D  A  L  S  U  R  H  M
O  A  D  N  F  A  E  Z  O  A  J  Q  O  U  B
E  O  K  T  B  P  A  R  L  F  V  D  C  N  Y
R  V  W  T  P  L  I  V  B  A  R  W  A  K  E
M  I  A  A  E  F  N  S  I  E  V  I  S  Y  Q
T  T  R  C  I  R  S  E  T  L  T  I  E  C  E
K  W  I  E  E  P  W  N  M  A  L  H  R  N  Z
W  O  D  T  I  V  E  T  W  O  Y  A  A  R  D
V  E  S  R  E  W  P  Z  G  V  Q  E  G  N  A
N  I  T  Z  B  C  T  H  I  D  U  E  D  E  Y
S  S  A  Z  X  A  S  I  C  K  O  K  M  Y  Y
```

57. Jesus Raises Lazarus from the Dead

ALWAYS	GRAVE	STONE
ARRIVAL	JUDEA	STRIPS
ASLEEP	LAZARUS	TOMB
BETHANY	LOUD	TWO
CAVE	ODOR	VILLAGE
FACE	SENT	VOICE
FOUR	SICK	WAKE
FRIEND	SISTER	WEPT
GLORIFIED	STAYED	WRAPPED

58.   Add to Your Faith

According as his <u>divine</u> power hath given unto us all things that <u>pertain</u> unto life and <u>godliness,</u> through the knowledge of him that hath called us to glory and <u>virtue.</u> hereby are given unto us exceeding great and <u>precious</u> promises: that by these ye might be <u>partakers</u> of the divine nature having escaped the corruption that is in the world through lust.

And <u>besides</u> this, giving all <u>diligence,</u> add to your faith virtue; and to virtue knowledge. And to knowledge <u>temperance</u>; and to temperance patience and to patience godliness; And to godliness brotherly <u>kindness</u>; and to brotherly kindness <u>charity</u>.

For if these things be in you, and <u>abound,</u> they make you that ye shall neither be <u>barren</u> not unfruitful in the knowledge of our Lord Jesus Christ. But he that <u>lack</u>eth these things is blind, and cannot see <u>afar</u> off. (2 Peter 1:3-9 KJV)

His divine power has given us everything we need for life and godliness through our knowledge of him, who called us by his own glory and <u>goodness</u>. Through these he has given us his very great and precious promises, so that through them you may <u>participate</u> in the divine nature and escape the corruption in the world caused by evil desires.

For this reason, make every <u>effort</u> to add to your faith goodness; and to goodness, knowledge; and to knowledge, <u>self-control</u>; and to self-control, perseverance; and to perseverance, godliness; and to godliness, brotherly kindness; and to brotherly kindness, <u>love</u>.

For if you <u>possess</u> these <u>qualities</u> in increasing measure, they will keep you from being ineffective and unproductive in your knowledge of our Lord Jesus Christ. But if anyone does not have them, he is nearsighted and blind, and has <u>forgotten</u> that he has been cleansed from his past sins.

Therefore, my brothers, be all the more <u>eager</u> to make your calling and <u>election</u> <u>sure</u>. For if you do these things, you will never fall, and you will receive a <u>rich</u> welcome into the eternal kingdom of our Lord and Savior Jesus Christ. (2 Peter 1:3-11 NIV)

```
N R L C G O O D N E S S P E D
V E A O O S A V I O R A A N D
Q I R F V N N L J C R G U N I
L S R R A E T M P T E O C P L
N E S T A T P R I R B J B A I
E I E T U B E C O A D X S R G
T T L R R E I M N L A C K T E
T I F P R P C N P I X X I A N
O L L P A H S V O E A L Z K C
G A X T A S E T E I R T I E E
R U E R E D R N G N T A R R T
O Q I S I O T X Z I I C N E X
F T S S F S U R E H C V E C P
Y O E F S S E N D N I K I L E
P B E Z S S E N I L D O G D E
```

58.Add to Your Faith

ABOUND	EFFORT	PARTICIPATE
AFAR	ELECTION	PERTAIN
BARREN	FORGOTTEN	POSSESS
BESIDE	GODLINESS	QUALITIES
CHARITY	GOODNESS	SAVIOR
CONTROL	KINDNESS	SELF
DILIGENCE	LACK	SURE
DIVINE	LOVE	TEMPERANCE
EAGER	PARTAKER	VIRTUE

59. Fruit of the Spirit

But the fruit of the Spirit is <u>love</u>, <u>joy</u>, <u>peace</u>, <u>long</u>-suffering, gentleness, goodness, <u>faith</u>, <u>meek</u>ness, <u>temperance</u>, against such there is no law. And they that are Christ's have <u>crucified</u> the flesh with the <u>affection</u> and <u>lusts</u>. If we live by the Spirit, let us also <u>walk</u> by the Spirit. Let us not be <u>desirous</u> of <u>vain</u>-glory, <u>provoking</u> one another, <u>envy</u>ing one <u>another</u>. (Galatians 5:22-26 KJV)

But the fruit of the Spirit is love, joy, peace, <u>patience</u>, <u>kindness</u>, goodness, <u>faithfulness</u>, gentleness, and self-control. Against such things there is no <u>law</u>. Those who belong to Christ Jesus have crucified the sinful nature with its <u>passions</u> and desires. Since we <u>live</u> by the Spirit let us keep in <u>step</u> with the Spirit. Let us not <u>become</u> <u>conceited</u>, provoking and <u>envying</u> each other. (Galatians 5:22-26 NIV)

```
C F P L L A W W A L K H E P M
R A A E O A L D N W H M V Q G
U N S I A N N W T G O O F P N
C O A S T C G Z E C J H M A I
I T N T E H E N E B E E E S R
F H I E V N T B L O X U E S E
I E A P L L L S E U D P K I F
E R V I E G O U U D S T X O F
D R V N L N P Q F O L T K N U
A E E O W L O V E H R H C Z S
F S R J K Y V N E G T I L R T
S Y G N I K O V O R P I S O Z
C O N C I E T E D C Q Q A E J
A F F E C T I O N G O O D F D
T E M P E R A N C E R P J O Y
```

59. Fruit of the Spirit

AFFECTION	GENTLENESS	MEEK
ANOTHER	GLORY	PASSION
BECOME	GOOD	PEACE
CONCEITED	JOY	PROVOKING
CRUCIFIED	LAW	STEP
DESIROUS	LIVE	SUFFERING
ENVY	LONG	TEMPERANCE
FAITH	LOVE	VAIN
FAITHFULNESS	LUST	WALK

60. The Truth

"I am the way, the <u>truth,</u> and the life: no man <u>come</u>th unto the <u>Father,</u> but by me. If ye had <u>known</u> me, ye should have known my Father also: and from henceforth, ye know him and have <u>seen</u> him....Believest that not that I am in the Father, and the Father in me? The words I <u>speak</u> unto you I speak not of <u>myself</u>: but the Father that <u>dwell</u>eth in me, he <u>doeth</u> the works." (John 14:5-6, 10 KJV)

"If ye <u>continue</u> in my word, then are ye my disciples indeed: And ye shall know the truth and the truth shall make you free." (John 8:31-32 KJV)

"If ye love me, keep my commandments. And I <u>pray</u> the Father and he shall give you another <u>Comforter</u>, that he may <u>abide</u> with you forever.

Even the Spirit of Truth; whom the world cannot receive because it seeth him not, <u>neither</u> knoweth him: but ye know him; for he dwelleth with you, and shall be in you." (John 14:14:17 KJV)

"I have much more to say to you, more than you can now <u>bear</u>. But when the Spirit of Truth, comes, he will guide you into all truth. He will not speak on his own; he will speak only what he <u>hears,</u> and he will tell you what is yet to come. He <u>will</u> <u>bring</u> <u>glory</u> to me by <u>taking</u> from what is mine and making it known to you. All that belongs to the Father is <u>mine</u>. That is why I said the Spirit will take from what is mine and make it known to you." (John 16:12-15 NIV)

"But the <u>hour</u> cometh, and now is, when the true worshippers shall worship the Father in spirit and in truth: for the Father <u>seeketh</u> such to worship him. God is Spirit: and they that worship him must worship him in spirit and in truth." (John 4:23-24 KJV)

"They are not of the world, even as I am not of the world. <u>Sanctify</u> them <u>through</u> thy truth: thy word is truth. As thou hast sent me into the world, even so have I also sent them in the world. And for their <u>sakes</u> I sanctify myself, that they also might be sanctified through the truth." (John 17:16-19 KJV)

```
S A N C T I F Y K N O W N G Q
M I N E Z G X B Q R A E B T R
T R Q F A S E E K G O Q E C M
S R S E E N S T H R O U G H F
H A U O E D I B A T H G L X F
C S K T S P E A K J H Q F A N
X O R E H D O S F T R L T E C
D W M A S S W D E K E H I O P
T M K F E E M O C S E T N Z R
B A A H O H D B Y R H T S Y A
L R K K L R D M C E I F M J Y
L L I I I K T J R N Y R O L G
F W E N N N O E U P T L F L V
I Q A W G G G E R V Q O N I E
F C V N D H O U R Y N C L W Q
```

60. The Truth

ABIDE	GLORY	SAKES
BEAR	HEARS	SANCTIFY
BRING	HOUR	SEEK
COME	KNOWN	SEEN
COMFORTER	MAKING	SPEAK
CONTINUE	MINE	TAKING
DOETH	MYSELF	THROUGH
DWELL	NEITHER	TRUTH
FATHER	PRAY	WILL

61. Jesus Christ (Other Names for)

Prince of Peace (Isaiah 9:6)
Messias (John 1:41)
Only Begotten Son (John 3:16)
Jesus of Nazareth (John 1:45)
Christ of God (Luke 23:35)
Son of Joseph (John 1:45)
Son of Man (John 1:51)
Rabbi (John 1:38)
Teacher (John 1:38)
Savior (John 4:42)
Author and finisher of our faith (Hebrews 12:2)
Sat down at the right hand of the Majesty on High
        (Hebrews 1:3)
Crucified (John 19:23)
Son of God (John 1:49)
King of Israel (John 1:51)
Lamb of God (John 1:36)
Son of David (Mark 10:47)
Master (Luke 17:13)
Chosen One (Luke 23:35)
The one whom God has sent (John 3:34)
I am the true vine (John 15:1)
No reputation, servant, humble (Philipians 2:7,8)
Firstborn among many brethren (Romans 8:29)
Resurrection and the Life (John11:25)
The One Moses wrote about (John 1:45)
High Priest (Hebrews 4:15)
I am the way, the truth, and the life. (John 14:6)
Tender Plant, root of dry ground (Isaiah 53:2)
Lord of lords (1 Timothy 6:15)
He ever liveth to make intercession for them.
        (Hebrews 7:25)

```
F  O  U  H  P  P  I  C  S  A  I  S  S  E  M
I  N  B  N  T  E  A  C  H  E  R  E  R  H  O
N  M  R  V  K  T  R  U  E  N  E  S  O  H  C
I  A  N  O  J  L  J  O  S  E  P  H  E  W  J
S  J  I  O  B  I  P  R  I  E  S  T  N  F  D
H  E  E  H  I  T  B  Y  V  W  L  S  I  A  P
E  S  V  G  U  S  S  B  M  A  L  Y  V  L  D
R  T  K  I  N  G  S  R  A  L  T  I  A  E  I
J  Y  G  H  R  B  S  E  I  R  D  N  I  H  R
R  X  R  D  E  F  O  Q  C  F  T  F  X  P  I
O  O  O  N  T  P  N  M  K  R  I  Y  P  E  K
I  G  H  U  S  L  X  Q  R  C  E  W  W  A  Y
V  N  T  O  A  O  K  O  U  T  G  T  H  M  I
A  B  U  R  M  C  O  R  E  N  Y  A  N  O  O
S  I  A  G  T  T  C  R  E  D  N  E  T  I  M
```

61.Jesus Christ (Other Names for)

AUTHOR	JOSEPH	ROOT
CHOSEN	KING	SAVIOR
CRUCIFIED	LAMB	SON
DAVID	MAJESTY	TEACHER
FINISHER	MASTER	TENDER
FIRSTBORN	MESSIAS	TRUE
GROUND	PLANT	VINE
HIGH	PRIEST	WAY
INTERCESSION	RABBI	WHOM

62.   The End of This Age

"At that time many will <u>turn</u> away from the faith and <u>betray</u> and <u>hate</u> <u>each</u> other, and many <u>false</u> prophets will appear and deceive many people. Because of the increase of wickedness, the love of most will grow <u>cold</u>, but he who stands firm to the <u>end</u> will be saved. And this <u>gospel</u> of the kingdom will be preached in the whole world as a <u>testimony</u> to all nations, and then the end will come." (Matthew 24:10-14 NIV)

"Watch out that you are not deceived. For many will come in my name, <u>claiming</u>, 'I am he,' and, 'The time is near.' Do not follow them. When you hear of <u>wars</u> and <u>revolutions</u>, do not be <u>frightened</u>. These things must happen first, but the end will not come right away.

Nation will <u>rise</u> against nation, and kingdom against kingdom. There will be great <u>earthquakes</u>, <u>famines</u> and <u>pestilences</u> in various places, and fearful events and great <u>signs</u> from heaven.

But before all of this, they will lay hands on you and persecute you...

When you see Jerusalem being surrounded by armies, you will know that its desolation is near....

There will be signs in the <u>sun</u>, <u>moon</u> and <u>stars</u>. On the earth, nations will be in <u>anguish</u> and <u>perplexity</u> at the <u>roaring</u> and <u>tossing</u> of the sea. Men will faint from terror, <u>apprehensive</u> of what is coming on the world, for the heavenly <u>bodies</u> will be shaken.

At that time they will see the Son of Man coming in a <u>cloud</u> with power and great glory. When these things begin to take place, stand up and lift up your heads, because your redemption is <u>drawing</u> near." (Luke 21:8-12, 20, 23-28 NIV)

For the Son of Man in his day will be like the <u>lightening</u>, which <u>flashes</u> and lights up the sky from one end to the other. (Luke 17:24 NIV)

```
S  B  G  A  G  N  I  S  S  O  T  R  U  E  B
R  E  O  E  S  L  A  F  S  T  H  C  A  E  L
G  Y  H  D  A  M  N  E  R  E  A  F  T  E  C
N  N  D  S  I  R  C  T  A  Y  S  R  P  R  L
I  O  L  P  A  E  T  A  W  E  A  S  S  O  A
N  M  O  O  N  L  S  H  C  Y  O  P  T  A  I
E  I  C  M  F  X  F  N  Q  G  Q  L  X  R  M
T  T  U  R  N  E  D  H  U  S  U  N  I  I
H  S  N  T  D  L  R  N  S  S  A  S  C  N  N
G  E  Y  G  I  A  K  K  M  E  I  K  B  G  G
I  T  Z  T  W  C  L  O  U  D  N  U  E  V  N
L  T  S  I  G  N  S  Y  L  U  G  I  G  S  Y
X  E  N  C  W  G  N  I  R  A  O  R  M  N  I
P  G  R  E  V  O  L  U  T  I  O  N  S  A  A
D  I  M  S  D  E  N  E  T  H  G  I  R  F  F
```

62. The End of This Age

ANGUISH	FALSE	REVOLUTIONS
BETRAY	FAMINES	ROARING
BODIES	FLASHES	SIGNS
CLAIMING	FRIGHTENED	STARS
CLOUD	GOSPEL	SUN
COLD	HATE	TESTIMONY
DRAWING	LIGHTENING	TOSSING
EACH	MOON	TURN
EARTHQUAKES	PESTILENCES	WARS

63. Little Children

Then little <u>children</u> were <u>brought</u> to Jesus for him to <u>place</u> his hands on them and <u>pray</u> for them. But the disciples <u>rebuked</u> those who brought them. Jesus said, "Let the little children come to me, do not <u>hinder</u> them, for the kingdom of <u>heaven</u> belongs to such as <u>these</u>. When he had placed his <u>hands</u> on them, he <u>went</u> from there. (Matthew 19: 13-15 NIV)

At that time the disciples came to Jesus and <u>asked</u>, "Who is the <u>greatest</u> in the kingdom of heaven?" He called a little child and had him <u>stand</u> among them. And he said: "I <u>tell</u> you the truth, <u>unless</u> you change and become like little children, you will never enter the kingdom of heaven. Therefore, <u>whoever</u> humbles himself like this child is the greatest in the kingdom of heaven.

And whoever welcomes a little child like this in my name <u>welcomes</u> me. But if <u>anyone</u> causes one of these <u>little</u> ones who <u>believe</u> in me to sin, it would be <u>better</u> for him to have a <u>large</u> <u>millstone</u> <u>hung</u> around his <u>neck</u> and be <u>drowned</u> in the <u>depths</u> of the sea." (Matthew 18:1-6 NIV)

```
O F Y Q J E U P W X H J N H K
V I X D L N R H X E I S E U S
Q A M T E E O D V J M L C N O
P G T V T E R E T I N L K G Q
J I A T V O I S L S N E B K E
L E E E W L E L R A H T O X C
H B R N E T S C T E N T Z Z A
W M E B A T Q W H H B Y P I L
E D W E O S T T E I G U O E P
N O R N S U R S R L L U K N D
T G E E H A N D S E C D O E E
V O L J I Y A R P S D O R R D
H N S T A N D S F J V N M E B
U G M L B Z E G R A L I I E N
A S K E D T H E S E E R K H S
```

63. Little Children

ANYONE	HANDS	PRAY
ASKED	HEAVEN	REBUKED
BELIEVE	HINDER	STAND
BETTER	HUNG	TELL
BROUGHT	LARGE	THESE
CHILDREN	LITTLE	UNLESS
DEPTHS	MILLSTONE	WELCOMES
DROWNED	NECK	WENT
GREATEST	PLACE	WHOEVER

64. Maturing in Christ

When I was a child, I <u>talk</u>ed like a child, I thought like a child, I <u>reason</u>ed like a child. When I became a man, I put <u>childish</u> <u>ways</u> behind me. (1 Corinthians 13:11 NIV)

Brothers, I could not <u>address</u> you as spiritual but as worldly – mere <u>infant</u>s in Christ. I gave you <u>milk</u>, not <u>solid</u> <u>food</u>, for you were not yet ready for it. Indeed, you still are not ready. You are still worldly. For since there is <u>jealousy</u> and quarreling among you, are you not worldly? Are you not <u>acting</u> like mere men? For when one says, "I follow Paul." And another, " follow Apollos," are you not mere men? What, after all is <u>Apollos</u>? And what is Paul" Only servant , through whom you came to believe –as the Lord has <u>assign</u>ed to each his task. I <u>plant</u>ed the seed, Apollos <u>watered</u> it, but God made it grow. (1 Corinthians 3:2-6 NIV)

We have much to say about this, but it is hard to <u>explain</u> because you are slow to learn. In fact, though you need someone to teach you the <u>elementary</u> truths of God's word all over again. You need milk, not solid food! Anyone who lives on milk, being still an infant, is not <u>acquaint</u>ed with the teaching about righteousness. But solid food is for the <u>mature</u>, who by <u>constant</u> use have trained themselves to distinguish good from evil.

Therefore let us have <u>leave</u> the elementary teachings about Christ and go on to maturity, not <u>laying</u> again the foundation of <u>repentance</u> from acts that lead to death, and of faith in God, <u>instruction</u> about <u>baptism</u>s, the laying on of hands, the resurrection of the dead, and eternal <u>judgment</u>. And God <u>permitting</u>, we will do so. (Hebrews 5:11-6:3 NIV)

```
T N S P E R M I T T I N G S A
E N J O J E A L O U S Y O C P
N G I V L F R E T A W L T N E
J O N A I L E Y N U I I O L C
U L S I U N O X V D N M E P H
D E U A Y Q S P P G P M T L I
G A W X E A C T A L E V A A L
E V S E C R L A R N A H L N D
M E Y R T E B S T U C I K T I
E P A E R A S A T N C M N C S
N N W U P E R N W D G T Y S H
T A T T R Y A M I L K I I H C
M A I D S F F O O D I J S O E
M S D D N T N A T S N O C S N
M A M I R E P E N T A N C E A
```

64.Maturing in Christ

ACQUAINT	EXPLAIN	MILK
ACTING	FOOD	PERMITTING
ADDRESS	INFANT	PLANT
APOLLOS	INSTRUCTION	REASON
ASSIGN	JEALOUSY	REPENTANCE
BAPTISM	JUDGMENT	SOLID
CHILDISH	LAYING	TALK
CONSTANT	LEAVE	WATER
ELEMENTARY	MATURE	WAYS

65. John The Baptist

There was in the days of Herod, the king of Judea, a certain priest name Zechariah…they had no child because that Elisabeth was barren, and they were now well stricken in years…Then an angel of the Lord [Gabriel, v. 19] appeared to him…"thy wife Elizabeth shall bear thee a son, and thou shalt call his name John. And thou shall have joy and gladness…he shall be filled with the Holy Ghost, even from his mother's womb…in the spirit and power of Elijah" (Luke 1:5, 7, 11, 13, 15, 17, 19 KJV)

John the Baptist came preaching in the Desert of Judea and saying, "Repent for the kingdom of heaven is near." This is he who was spoken of through the prophet Isaiah:

"A voice of one calling in the desert,

Prepare the way for the Lord,

  Make straight paths for him." [Isaiah 40:3]

John's clothes were made of camel's hair, and he had a leather belt around his waist. His food was locusts and wild honey. People went out to him from Jerusalem and all Judea and the whole region of the Jordan. Confessing their sins, they were baptized by him in the Jordan River.

I will baptize you with water for repentance. But after me will come one who is more powerful than I, whose sandals I am not fit to carry. He will baptize you with the Holy Spirit and with fire.

Then Jesus came from Galilee to the Jordan to be baptized by John. But John tried to deter him, saying, "I need to be baptized by you, and do you come to me?" Jesus replied, "Let it be so now, it is proper for us to do this to fulfill all righteousness." Then John consented. (Matthew 3:1-6, 11, 13-15 NIV)

Then there arose a question between some of John's disciples and the Jews about purifying. And they came unto John and said unto him, Rabbi, he that was with thee beyond Jordan, to whom thou barest witness, behold, the same baptizeth, and all men come to him.

John answered and said, "A man can receive nothing except it be given him from heaven…I said I am not the Christ, but that I am sent before him…my joy is therefore fulfilled. He must increase, but, I must decrease." (John 3:25-26, 27, 28, 29-30 KJV)

```
C  B  C  R  L  N  B  D  H  P  D  X  C  O  K
V  H  I  E  E  A  E  T  W  V  J  O  H  N  G
S  A  G  R  P  C  E  Q  J  A  O  U  O  C  S
H  N  R  T  R  B  I  I  L  U  I  T  T  Z  S
A  A  I  E  A  Z  G  K  E  V  D  S  G  Z  E
B  Z  A  Z  G  P  E  L  L  H  L  E  T  K  N
E  S  I  H  A  O  Y  C  A  E  A  E  A  V  T
E  L  O  T  U  I  L  R  H  D  I  J  M  L  I
E  S  H  T  N  E  P  E  R  A  N  R  I  A  W
T  S  I  S  A  I  A  H  S  F  R  E  B  L  C
P  R  E  P  A  R  E  X  F  X  S  I  S  A  E
J  F  X  E  Y  S  T  S  U  C  O  L  A  S  G
L  E  A  T  H  E  R  I  C  B  M  O  W  H  L
P  R  O  P  E  R  Y  N  O  I  T  S  E  U  Q
R  E  G  I  O  N  Y  N  E  K  C  I  R  T  S
```

65. John The Baptist

ANGEL	GLADNESS	PROPER
BAPTIZE	HAIR	QUESTION
BARREN	ISAIAH	REGION
CAMEL	JOHN	REPENT
DECREASE	JUDEA	STRICKEN
ELIJAH	LEATHER	WAIST
ELIZABETH	LOCUSTS	WITNESS
GABRIEL	PATHS	WOMB
GHOST	PREPARE	ZECHARIAH

66. Animals in the Bible

Antelope	(Deuteronomy 14:4)
Ass	(Genesis 22:3)
Bat	(Genesis 14:18)
Birds	(Genesis 7:14)
Bull	(Isaiah 51:20)
Camel	(Genesis 30:43)
Cattle	(Genesis 1:14)
Cock	(Luke 22:61)
Coney	(Deuteronomy 14:7)
Cow	(Leviticus 22:28)
Deer	(Deuteronomy 14:5)
Donkey	(John 12:15)
Dove	(Matthew 3:16)
Eagle	(Isaiah 40:31)
Ewe	(Genesis 21:28)
Fallon	(Genesis 14:13)
Foul	(Genesis 7:21)
Gazelle	(Deuteronomy 14:4)
Goat	(Genesis 30:35)
Gull	(Genesis 14:14)
Hawk	(Genesis 14:15)
Lamb	(Genesis 30:35)
Lion	(Judge 14:8)
Owl	(Genesis 14:16)
Oxen	(Genesis 12:16)
Pelican	(Leviticus 11:18)
Pig	(Genesis 14:8)
Pigeon	(Genesis 15:9)
Rabbit	(Deuteronomy 14:7)
Raven	(Genesis 14:14)
Scorpions	(Luke 10:19)
Serpent	(Genesis 3:1)
Sheep	(Genesis 12:16)
Stork	(Genesis 14:18)
Viper	(Acts 28:3)
Wolf	(Isaiah 65:25)

```
E  A  C  L  C  L  F  C  A  J  W  O  C  L  A
V  E  L  A  W  A  A  P  E  H  P  R  A  M  S
F  U  M  Q  L  T  E  P  D  E  A  M  U  S  S
B  E  M  L  T  L  O  C  C  O  B  W  W  L  Y
L  X  O  L  I  L  F  B  O  O  V  T  K  W  W
Q  N  E  C  E  W  O  E  I  N  C  E  A  O  G
L  M  A  T  S  M  U  O  Y  R  E  K  V  O  R
L  N  N  D  L  N  L  B  O  T  D  Y  P  Y  G
T  A  E  R  O  I  O  E  T  Y  I  S  G  A  Q
N  E  V  A  R  J  O  I  L  N  E  B  R  N  A
R  T  L  L  U  G  U  N  P  L  E  K  B  L  E
X  S  V  I  P  E  R  R  V  R  E  P  N  A  C
C  H  E  W  E  K  R  O  T  S  O  Z  R  O  R
W  V  O  T  A  B  P  E  E  H  S  C  A  E  D
E  A  G  L  E  W  O  L  F  T  Q  F  S  G  S
```

66.Animals in the Bible

ANTELOPE	CONEY	FOUL	RABBIT
ASS	COW	GOAT	RAVEN
BAT	DEER	GULL	SCORPIONS
BIRDS	DONKEY	HAWK	SERPENT
BULL	DOVE	LAMB	SHEEP
CAMEL	EAGLE	LION	STORK
CATTLE	EWE	OWL	VIPER
COCK	FALLON	PELICAN	WOLF

67. Cain and Abel

And Adam knew Eve his wife: and she conceived, and <u>bare</u> <u>Cain</u>, and said, I have <u>gotten</u> a man from the Lord. And she again bare his brother <u>Abel</u>. And Abel was a <u>keeper</u> of sheep, but Cain was a <u>tiller</u> of the <u>ground</u>. And in the <u>process</u> of time it came to pass, that Cain brought of the fruit of the ground an <u>offering</u> unto the Lord. And Abel he also brought of the <u>fristlings</u>, of his <u>flock</u> and of the <u>fat</u> thereof. And the Lord had <u>respect</u> unto Able and to his offering: But unto Cain and his offering he had no respect. And Cain was very <u>wroth</u>, and his countenance fell.

And the Lord said unto Cain, Why art thou wroth? And why is thy countenance fallen? If thou does well, shalt thou not be accepted? And if thou doest not well, sin lieth at the door. And unto thee shall be his desire, and thou shall <u>rule</u> over him.

An Cain talked with Abel his brother: and it came to pass, when they were in the <u>field</u>, that Cain rose up against Abel his brother, and <u>slew</u> him. And the Lord came to Cain, Where is Abel thy brother? And he said, I know not: Am I my brother's keeper? And he said, What hast thou done? The <u>voice</u> of thy brother's <u>blood</u> <u>crieth</u> unto me form the ground. And now are thou cursed from the earth, which hath <u>opened</u> her mouth to receive thy brother's blood from thy <u>hand;</u> When thou tillest the ground, it shall not henceforth <u>yield</u> unto thee her strength; a <u>fugitive</u> and a <u>vagabond</u> shalt thou be in the earth.

And Cain said unto the Lord, My punishment is greater that I can <u>bear</u>. Behold, thou hast <u>driven</u> me out this day from the face of the earth; and from the face shall I be hid... everyone findeth me shall slay me. And the Lord said unto him, Therefore whosoever slayeth Cain, vengeance shall be taken on him <u>sevenfold</u>....And Cain went our from the presence of the Lord, and dwelt in the land of <u>Nod</u>, on the east of Eden. (Genesis 4:1-13, 14, 15-16 KJV)

```
D  T  D  C  D  K  T  A  V  W  L  F  N  O  D
Y  L  E  N  T  R  E  I  J  O  X  L  Z  L  N
I  A  O  V  O  C  I  E  L  L  I  O  T  X  G
E  B  M  F  I  B  E  V  P  L  C  C  O  Y  H
L  E  J  G  N  T  A  P  E  E  E  K  E  F  L
D  L  P  R  V  E  I  G  S  N  R  R  N  G  F
J  F  I  E  L  D  V  G  A  E  G  N  N  I  C
T  J  T  W  W  A  G  E  U  V  R  I  R  C  C
C  G  A  P  W  E  L  S  S  F  R  S  S  R  N
G  F  F  N  V  R  A  E  B  E  T  S  I  N  O
O  I  E  I  L  N  H  H  F  L  E  E  E  P  D
K  E  R  A  R  T  E  F  I  C  T  T  E  O  H
V  L  A  C  O  T  O  N  O  H  T  N  O  X  K
H  U  B  R  F  D  G  R  D  O  E  L  G  K  I
E  R  W  E  J  S  P  B  G  D  B  L  A  F  W
```

67.Cain and Abel

ABEL	FIRSTLINGS	RESPECT
BARE	FLOCK	RULE
BEAR	FUGITIVE	SEVENFOLD
BLOOD	GOTTEN	SLEW
CAIN	KEEPER	TILLER
CRIETH	NOD	VAGABOND
DRIVEN	OFFERING	VOICE
FAT	OPENED	WROTH
FIELD	PROCESS	YIELD

68. What is Man?

When I consider thy heavens, the work of thy fingers, the moon and the stars, which thou hast ordained:

What is man, that thou art mindful of him? and the son of man, that thou visitest him?

For thou has made him a little lower that the angels, and has crowned him with glory and honor.

Thou has madest him to have dominion over the works of thy hands; thou hast put all things under his feet... (Psalm 8:3-6 KJV)

And God said, Let us make man in our image, after our likeness: and let them have dominion over the fish of the sea, and over the fowl of the air, and over the cattle, and over all the earth, and over every creeping thing that creepeth upon the earth.

So God created man in his own image, in the image of God created he him, male and female created he them.

And God blessed them, and God said unto them, Be fruitful, and multiply, and replenish the earth, and subdue it: and have dominion ...(Genesis 1:26-28 KJV)

And the Lord formed man of the dust of the ground, and breathed into his nostrils the breath of life; and man became a living soul. And God planted a garden eastward in Eden; and there he put the man whom he had formed.

And the Lord took the man, and put him into the garden of Eden to dress it and to keep it. And the Lord commanded the man, saying, Of every tree of the garden thou mayest freely eat; But of the tree of the knowledge of good and evil, thous shalt not eat ot it: for in the day that thou eatest thereof thou shalt surely die.

And the Lord said, it is not good that man should be alone; I will make him an help meet for him...And the Lord God caused a deep sleep to fall upon Adam, and he slept: and he took one of his ribs, and closed up the flesh instead thereof; And the rib, which the Lord God had taken from man, made he a woman, and brought her unto man. And Adam said, This is now bone of my bones, and flesh of my flesh: she shall be called Woman, because she was taken out of Man.

Therefore shall a man leave his father and his mother, and cleave unto his wife: and they shall be one flesh. (Genesis 2:7, 15, 18, 21-25 KJV)

```
Y O F M S Y B P O F S W C C C
Y R I O X A S R R E L R C S U
L D S O F L B E E E U E A M Q
P A H N Y T P R D A L D S T C
I I M U S L E C S E T A B H S
T N K C E D D M C R T H M U X
L E Y N I E R T F S E A E E S
U D I S N E C L L J V G E D F
M S N W V D G E I U I I N R Y
H O O A E X P S S B I R S I C
C R E M S T R M L E L A M I F
C L R S B E N O S T R I L S T
C O E O D L I K E N E S S E W
F R N N D O M I N I O N H M J
D E U D L D N G N I P E E R C
```

68. What is Man?

BONE	FEMALE	NOSTRILS
BREATHED	FINGERS	ORDAINED
CLEAVE	FISH	REPLENISH
CONSIDER	FLESH	RIBS
CREATED	FORMED	SLEPT
CREEPING	LIKENESS	STARS
CROWNED	MALE	SUBDUE
DOMINION	MOON	UNDER
DRESS	MULTIPLY	VISIT

69. Peter

When Jesus came into the <u>coasts</u> of Caesarea Philippi, he asked his disciples, saying, "Whom do men say that I am?" And they said, Some say that thou art John the Baptist: some say Elijah; and others, Jeremiah, or one of the prophets. He saith unto them, "But whom do ye say I am?" And <u>Simon</u> Peter answered and said, Thou art Christ, the son of the <u>living</u> God. And Jesus answered and said unto him, "Blessed art thou, Simon <u>Barjona</u>: for flesh and blood hath not revealed it unto thee, but my father which is in heaven. And I say unto thee, That thou art Peter, and upon this <u>rock</u> (of revelation) I will <u>build</u> my <u>church</u>; and the <u>gates</u> of <u>hell</u> shall not <u>prevail</u> against it. And I will give unto thee the <u>keys</u> of the Kingdom of heaven. (Matthew 16:13-19a KJV)

And when Jesus came unto Peter's house, he saw his wife's mother laid, and sick of a <u>fever</u>. And he touched her hand, and the fever left her: and she <u>arose,</u> and ministered unto them. (Matthew 8:14-16 KJV)

And when the disciples saw him <u>walking</u> on the sea, they were troubled, saying it is a spirit; and they cried out for fear. But straightway Jesus spake unto them, saying "Be of good cheer; it is I; be not afraid." And Peter answered him and said, Lord, if it be thou, bid me come unto thee on the <u>water</u>. And he said, "Come." And when Peter was come out of the ship, he walked on the water, to go to Jesus. But when he saw the <u>wind</u> boisterous, he was afraid; and beginning to sink, he cried, saying, Lord, save me. And immediately Jesus stretched forth his hand, and caught him, and said unto him, "O thou of little faith, wherefore didst thou doubt?" (Matthew 14:26-31 KJV)

Jesus [began] to show unto his disciples, how that he must go unto Jerusalem, and <u>suffer</u> many things of the <u>elders</u> and chief priest and <u>scribes,</u> and be killed, and be <u>raised</u> again the <u>third</u> day. Then Peter took him, and began to rebuke him, saying, Be it far from thee, Lord: this shall not be unto thee. But he turned, and said unto Peter, "Get thee behind me, Satan: thou art an offense unto me: for thou <u>savorest</u> not the things that be of God, but those that be of men." (Matthew 16:21-23 KJV)

And after a while came unto him they that stood by, and said to Peter, Surely thou art one of them; for thy speech betrayeth thee. Then began he to curse and to <u>swear,</u> saying, I know not the man. And immediately the cock crew. And Peter remembered the word of Jesus, which said unto him, Before the <u>crow,</u> thou shalt deny me thrice. And he went out, and <u>wept</u> bitterly. (Matthew 26:73-75 KJV)

Then Peter said unto them, <u>Repent,</u> and be baptized everyone of you in the name of Jesus Christ for the remission of sins and ye shall receive the gift of the Holy Ghost. For the <u>promise</u> is unto you, and to your children, and to all that are afar off, even as many as the Lord our God shall call. And with many other words did he testify and <u>exhort,</u> saying, Save yourselves from this untoward generation. Then they that <u>gladly</u> received his word were baptized: and the same day there were added unto them about <u>three</u> thousand. (Acts 2:38-41 KJV)

```
H  M  C  W  A  T  E  R  N  L  M  W  W  F  E
N  C  W  Q  W  I  N  D  O  C  L  A  M  X  T
T  O  R  Q  F  E  V  E  R  I  L  Q  H  R  H
H  H  M  U  L  D  H  C  A  K  P  O  E  J  I
R  E  W  I  H  P  F  V  I  L  R  F  D  R  R
E  L  Q  T  S  C  E  N  T  T  F  D  O  M  D
E  L  C  I  A  R  G  R  R  U  B  U  I  L  D
J  X  W  T  P  N  X  Z  S  E  A  U  P  S  E
G  A  T  E  S  O  O  S  U  Y  P  R  A  Y  G
F  G  F  A  R  H  P  J  E  S  L  E  H  E  T
D  G  N  I  V  I  L  K  R  B  R  D  N  K  P
Y  R  E  H  J  E  S  O  R  A  I  E  A  T  E
E  F  O  R  S  T  S  A  O  C  B  R  D  L  W
M  G  E  C  R  O  W  X  F  J  A  X  C  L  G
M  V  U  C  K  J  W  E  R  A  E  W  S  S  E
```

69.Peter

AROSE	GATES	SIMON
BARJONA	GLADLY	SUFFER
BUILD	HELL	SWEAR
CHURCH	KEYS	THIRD
COASTS	LIVING	THREE
CROW	PREVAIL	WALKING
ELDERS	REPENT	WATER
EXHORT	ROCK	WEPT
FEVER	SCRIBES	WIND

70. Who's In Charge?

What then shall we say? Is God <u>unjust</u>? Not at all! For he says to Moses, I will have <u>mercy</u> on whom I have mercy, and I will have compassion on whom I have compassion.

It does not, <u>therefore,</u> <u>depend</u> on man's <u>desire</u> or <u>effort</u>, but on God's mercy. For the <u>Scripture</u> says to <u>Pharaoh</u>: "I raised you up for this <u>purpose</u>, that I might <u>display</u> my power in you and that my name might be proclaimed in all the earth. Therefore God has mercy on whom he wants to have mercy, and he <u>hardens</u> whom he wants to harden.

One of you will say to me: "Then why does God still blame us? For who <u>resists</u> his will?" But who are you, O man, to talk back to God? "Shall what is formed say to him who formed it, 'Why did you make me like this?'" Does not the <u>potter</u> have the right to make out of the same <u>lump</u> of <u>clay</u> some pottery for <u>noble</u> purposes and some for <u>common</u> use? (Romans 9:14-21 NIV)

The Lord <u>works</u> out everything for his own ends---even the wicked for a day of <u>disaster</u>. (Proverbs 16:4 NIV)

See, it is I who created the <u>blacksmith</u> who fans the <u>coals</u> into <u>flame</u> and <u>forges</u> a <u>weapon</u> <u>fit</u> for its work. And it is I who have created the <u>destroyer</u> to work <u>havoc</u>; no weapon forged against you will prevail. (Isaish 54:16-17 NIV)

"…for without me ye can do nothing." (John 15:5 KJV)

"A man can receive nothing, except it be given him from heaven. (John 3:27 KJV)

```
B D S T H E R E F O R E H D S
P L I E Q G X E M A L F N N W
R H A S G P S K R O W E E D P
K H A C P R C L A Y P D E O T
R A M R K L O M D E R S T F J
E V E Q A S A F D A T T P T C
T O R A S O M Y H R E O M O S
S C C R T N H I O R M H U B T
A G Y N O E P Y T N O B L E S
S K K P F U E U E H O P I V I
I C A F R R E J N R E M U W S
D E O P C W T I F J I D M I E
W R O Q U F W G O O U S T O R
T S C O A L S C V V R S E N C
E S T E R U T P I R C S T D N
```

70. Who's In Charge?

BLACKSMITH	EFFORT	PHARAOH
CLAY	FIT	POTTER
COALS	FLAME	PURPOSE
COMMON	FORGES	RESISTS
DEPEND	HARDENS	SCRIPTURE
DESIRE	HAVOC	THEREFORE
DESTROYER	LUMP	UNJUST
DISASTER	MERCY	WEAPON
DISPLAY	NOBLE	WORKS

71. The Holy Spirit

"And I will pray the Father, and he shall give you <u>another</u> <u>Comforter</u>, that he may <u>abide</u> with you forever; Even the Spirit of Truth, whom the world cannot receive, because it seeth him not, neither knoweth him: but ye know him; for he dwelleth with you, and shall be in you. I will not leave you <u>comfortless</u>: I will come to you. Yet a little while, and the world <u>seeth</u> me no more, but ye see me: because I live, ye shall live also. At that day ye shall know that I am in my Father, and ye in me and I in you... If a man love me, he will <u>keep</u> my <u>words</u>: and my Father will love him, and we will <u>come</u> unto him, and make our <u>abode</u> with him... But the Comforter, which is the Holy Ghost, whom the Father shall send in my name, he shall <u>teach</u> you all things, and bring all things to your remembrance; whatsoever I have said unto you." (John 14:16-20, 23, 26 KJV)

"Nevertheless, I tell you the truth: it is <u>expedient</u> for you that I go away: for if I go not away, the Comforter will not come unto you, but if I <u>depart,</u> I will send him unto you. And when he come, he will <u>reprove</u> the world of sin, and of righteousness, and of <u>judgment</u>... I have yet many things to say unto you, but ye cannot bear them now. <u>Howbeit</u> when he, the Spirit of truth is come, he will guide you into all truth: for he shall not speak of <u>himself;</u> but whatsoever he shall hear, that he <u>speak</u>: and he will <u>show</u> you things to come. He will <u>glorify</u> me: for he shall receive of <u>mine,</u> and shall show it unto you. All things that the Father hath are mine: therefore said I that he shall take of mine, and shall show it unto you." (John 16:7-8, 12-15 KJV)

"...wait for the <u>promise</u> of the Father, which" saith he, "ye have heard of me. For John baptized with <u>water;</u> but ye shall be baptized with the <u>Holy</u> Ghost not many days <u>hence</u>... It is not for you to know the <u>times</u> or the <u>seasons,</u> which the Father hath put in his own power. But ye shall receive power, after that the Holy Ghost is come <u>upon</u> you: and ye shall be witnesses unto me both in Jerusalem, and in all Judea, and in <u>Samaria,</u> and unto the <u>uttermost</u> part of the earth." (Acts 1:4-5, 7-8 KJV)

```
J  G  G  S  A  M  A  R  I  A  Z  Q  W  A  H
F  U  L  R  K  E  E  P  V  V  S  A  H  I  A
P  N  D  O  Y  O  W  O  H  S  T  T  M  N  Q
E  R  I  G  R  M  V  H  P  E  E  S  O  C  C
X  R  O  S  M  I  H  O  R  E  E  T  C  O  P
P  W  Q  M  S  E  F  L  S  L  H  O  A  M  E
E  E  R  Y  I  E  N  Y  F  E  M  F  P  E  V
D  T  I  M  E  S  L  T  R  F  U  R  J  R  O
I  W  U  U  N  T  E  T  O  A  B  I  D  E  R
E  M  I  N  E  A  D  R  R  H  B  Y  K  H  P
N  Y  S  A  B  E  T  F  K  O  E  O  K  L  E
T  P  C  O  P  E  Z  T  L  A  F  N  K  P  R
A  H  D  A  R  W  O  R  D  S  E  M  C  Z  J
O  E  R  Y  S  N  O  S  A  E  S  P  O  E  M
J  T  J  T  S  O  M  R  E  T  T  U  S  C  F
```

71. The Holy Spirit

ABIDE	HENCE	SEASONS
ABODE	HIMSELF	SEETH
ANOTHER	HOLY	SHOW
COME	JUDGMENT	SPEAK
COMFORTER	KEEP	TEACH
COMFORTLESS	MINE	TIMES
DEPART	PROMISE	UTTERMOST
EXPEDIENT	REPROVE	WATER
GLORIFY	SAMARIA	WORDS

72. Spiritual Man

We do, however, speak a <u>message</u> of <u>wisdom</u> among the <u>mature</u>, but not the wisdom of this <u>age</u> or of the <u>rulers</u> of this age, who are <u>coming</u> to nothing. No, we speak of God's <u>secret</u> wisdom, a wisdom that has been <u>hidden</u> and God <u>destined</u> for our glory <u>before</u> time began. <u>None</u> of the rulers of this age understood it, for if they had, they would not have crucified the Lord of glory. However, as it is <u>written</u>:

No <u>eye</u> has <u>seen</u>,
no <u>ear</u> has <u>heard</u>,
no mind had <u>conceived</u>
what God has <u>prepared</u> for those
who love him. (Ref: Isaiah 64:4)

but God has revealed it to us by his Spirit.
The Spirit <u>searches</u> all things, even the deep things of God. For who among men knows the thoughts of a man except the man's spirit within him? In the same way no one knows the thoughts of God except the spirit of God. We have not received the spirit of the world but the Spirit who is from God, that we may understand what God has freely given us. This is what we speak, not in words taught us by human wisdom but in words taught by the Spirit, expressing <u>spiritual</u> truths in spiritual words. The man without the Spirit does not <u>accept</u> the things that come from the Spirit of God, for they are <u>foolishness</u> to him, and he cannot understand them, because they are spiritually <u>discerned</u>. The spiritual man makes judgments about all things, but he himself is not <u>subject</u> to any man's judgement:

For who knows the mind of the Lord
That he may <u>instruct</u> him? (Ref: Isaiah 40:13)
<u>But</u> we have the mind of Christ. (1 Corinthians 2:6-16 NIV)

```
H E A R D D U H H N B W E E D
F U Z T E N O N E E R G V E D
A G E M R F S D F I A I S E R
D S Z C X P D O T S E T R U W
W I S S G I R T S C I A L S I
R I S E H E E N N P E X E S
S E N C N N M O E E R Q E E D
S U V S E H C D R S S D P N O
W E B E T R S P C E I M T W M
X J C J A R N I T O R K U Q N
S D U R E L U E L P M U B I X
R E J M E C E C D O E I T L E
A Y G G B T T D T Q O C N A I
E E K S E H C R A E S F C G M
S P I R I T U A L J K T X A W
```

72. Spiritual Man

ACCEPT	EYE	REVEALED
AGE	FOOLISHNESS	RULERS
BEFORE	HEARD	SEARCHES
BUT	HIDDEN	SECRET
COMING	INSTRUCT	SEEN
CONCEIVED	MATURE	SPIRITUAL
DESTINED	MESSAGE	SUBJECT
DISCERNED	NONE	WISDOM
EAR	PREPARED	WRITTEN

73. Jacob Wrestles With God

That <u>night</u> Jacob got up and took his two <u>wives</u>, his <u>two</u> maidservants and his <u>eleven</u> <u>sons</u> and <u>crossed</u> the <u>ford</u> of the <u>Jabok</u>. After he had sent them <u>across</u> the <u>stream</u>, he sent <u>over</u> his possessions. So Jacob was left <u>alone</u>, and a man <u>wrestled</u> with him till <u>daybreak</u>. When the man saw that he could not <u>overpower</u> him, he touched the <u>socket</u> of Jacob's <u>hip</u> so that his hip was <u>wrenched</u> as he wrestled with the man. Then the man said, "Let me go, for it is daybreak."

But Jacob replied, "I will not let you go unless you bless me." The man asked him, "What is your name?" "Jacob," he answered.

Then the man said, "Your name will no <u>longer</u> be Jacob, but Israel (means: <u>struggles</u> with God), because you have struggled with God and with men and have over." Jacob said, "Please tell me your name." But he replied, "Why do you ask my name?" The he <u>blessed</u> him there. So Jacob called the place <u>Peniel</u> (means: face of God), saying, "It is because I saw God face to face and yet my life was <u>spared</u>."

The sun rose above him as he passed Peniel, and he was <u>limping</u> because of his hip. Therefore to this day the Israelites do not eat the <u>tendon</u> <u>attached</u> to the socket of the hip, because the socket of Jacob's hip was <u>touched</u> <u>near</u> the tendon.

(Genesis 32:22-32 NIV)

73.Jacob Wrestles With God

ACROSS	JABOK	SONS
ALONE	LIMPING	SPARED
ATTACHED	LONGER	STREAM
BLESSED	NEAR	STRUGGLES
CROSSED	NIGHT	TENDON
DAYBREAK	OVER	TOUCHED
ELEVEN	OVERPOWER	TWO
FORD	PENIEL	WIVES
HIP	SOCKET	WRESTLED

74. The Offspring of Abraham, Isaac and Jacob

Abram's wife was Sarai. (Genesis 11: 29 KJV)

And Sarai Abram's wife took Hagar her maid the Egyptian…and gave her to her husband Abram to be his wife. Abram was eighty-six years old when Hagar bore him Ishmael. (Genesis 16:3, 16 KJV)

Neither shall thy name anymore be called Abram, but thy name shall be Abraham; for a father of many nations have I made thee…As for Sarai thy wife, thou shall not call her name Sarai, but Sarah shall her name be. (Genesis 17: 5, 15 KJV)

Abraham called the name of his son that was born unto him, whom Sarah bare to him, Isaac. (Genesis 21:3 KJV)

Again Abraham took a wife, and her name was Keturah. And she bare him Simran, and Jokshan, and Medan, and Midian, and Ishbak, and Shuah. (Genesis 25:1-2 KJV)

And Isaac brought her into his mother Sarah's tent, and took Rebekah, and she became his wife… (Genesis 24:67 KJV) And the first to come out red, all over like a hairy garmet; and they called his name Esau. And after that came his brother out, and his hand took hold on Esau's heel; and his name was called Jacob. (Genesis 25:25-26 KJV)

Now the sons of Jacob were twelve: The sons of Leah: Rueben Jacob's firstborn, and Simeon, Levi, and Judah, and Issachar, and Zebulun. The sons of Rachel: Joseph and Benjamin. And the sons of Bilhah, Rachel's hand maid: Dan, and Napthali: And the sons of Zilpah, Leah's handmaid: Gad, and Asher:. (Genesis 35:22-26 KJV)

She (Leah) bare a daughter, and called her name Dinah (Genesis 30:21 KJV)

```
J  D  I  Q  A  N  M  I  C  J  R  I  N  P  D
G  Y  C  S  E  I  S  N  O  A  L  A  S  L  M
F  Y  H  B  D  H  U  K  H  A  R  F  H  Z  U
M  E  E  I  B  L  S  C  H  M  K  P  U  K  H
R  U  A  A  U  H  A  T  I  F  Q  E  A  G  A
R  N  K  B  A  S  P  S  Y  D  V  I  H  G  E
B  B  E  N  S  A  R  U  C  G  W  V  J  H  L
P  Z  E  I  N  I  J  A  J  H  B  E  Q  A  B
Y  D  C  N  I  H  V  O  C  N  A  L  Q  D  O
X  A  E  H  J  S  A  H  S  H  O  P  C  U  C
H  N  J  S  K  A  H  K  A  E  A  E  L  J  A
A  H  V  T  Q  F  M  M  E  H  P  L  M  I  J
N  O  D  D  L  R  L  I  A  B  L  H  B  I  Z
I  K  A  A  U  A  S  E  N  E  E  I  M  A  S
S  E  G  E  W  N  A  D  E  M  L  R  B  B  D
```

74. The Offspring of Abraham, Isaac & Jacob

ASHER	JACOB	RACHAL
BENJAMIN	JOKSHAN	REBEKAH
BILHAH	JOSEPH	RUEBEN
DAN	JUDAH	SHUAH
ESAU	LEAH	SIMEON
GAD	LEVI	SIMRAN
ISHBAK	MEDAN	SINAH
ISHMAEL	MIDIAN	ZEBULUN
ISSACHAR	NAPTHALI	ZILPAH

75. The Body is the Temple of the Spirit

"Everything is <u>permissible</u> for me" but not everything is <u>beneficial</u>, "Everything is permissible for me" – but I will not be <u>mastered</u> by <u>anything</u>. <u>Food</u> for the <u>stomach</u> and the stomach for food" – but God will <u>destroy</u> them both. The body is not <u>meant</u> for sexual <u>immorality</u>, but for the Lord, and the Lord for the <u>body</u>. By his <u>power</u> God <u>raised</u> the Lord from the dead, and he will raise us also. Do you not know that your <u>bodies</u> are <u>members</u> of Christ himself? Shall I then take the members of Christ and <u>unite</u> them with a prostitute? Never! Do you not know that he who unites himself with a prostitute is one with her in body? For it is said, "The two will <u>become</u> one <u>flesh</u>." But he who unites himself with the Lord is one with him in spirit.

Flee from sexual immorality. All other sins a man <u>commits</u> are <u>outside</u> his body, but he who sins sexually sins against his own body. Do you not know that your body is a <u>temple</u> of the <u>Holy Spirit</u>, who is in you, whom you have received from God? You are not your own, you were <u>brought</u> at a <u>price</u>. Therefore <u>honor</u> God with your body.

(1 Corinthians 6:12-20 NIV)

```
Y  T  I  M  M  O  R  A  L  I  T  Y  J  S  G
B  O  E  S  T  O  M  A  C  H  F  U  T  N  P
E  R  R  M  P  M  E  C  I  R  P  I  I  E  M
W  E  O  T  P  V  E  H  U  R  M  H  R  E  O
G  S  B  U  S  L  Z  Z  R  M  T  M  M  Q  U
D  O  O  B  G  E  E  Z  O  Y  I  B  D  V  T
E  O  D  J  E  H  D  C  N  S  E  U  E  V  S
R  T  Y  L  D  N  T  A  S  R  H  O  L  Y  I
E  N  X  Z  X  T  E  I  S  U  N  I  T  E  D
T  A  P  G  I  S  B  F  D  E  D  O  O  F  E
S  E  J  R  E  L  H  H  I  E  M  N  W  J  L
A  M  I  I  E  S  F  O  J  C  S  O  A  R  X
M  P  D  G  E  F  I  N  S  S  I  I  C  J  D
S  O  M  L  W  D  A  O  K  D  A  A  A  E  O
B  G  F  X  T  P  D  R  E  W  O  P  L  R  B
```

Copyright © GIL PUBLICATIONS 2004

75.The Body is the Temple of the Spirit

ANYTHING	FOOD	PERMISSIBLE
BECOME	HOLY	POWER
BENEFICIAL	HONOR	PRICE
BODIES	IMMORALITY	RAISED
BODY	MASTERED	SPIRIT
BROUGHT	MEANT	STOMACH
COMMITS	MEMBERS	TEMPLE
DESTROY	OUTSIDE	UNITE
FLESH		

76. Soldiers and Athletes

Endure <u>hardship</u> with us like a good <u>soldier</u> of Christ Jesus. No one serving as a soldier gets <u>involved</u> in <u>civilian</u> <u>affairs</u>—he wants to please his commanding <u>officer</u>. Similarly, if anyone <u>competes</u> as an <u>athlete</u>, he does not receive the <u>victor</u>'s <u>crown</u> unless he competes according to the <u>rules</u>. The hardworking farmer should be the first to receive a share of the <u>crops</u>. (2 Timothy 2:3-6 NIV)

Everyone who competes in the <u>games</u> goes into <u>strict</u> <u>training</u>. They do it to get a crown that will not last; but we do it to get a crown that will last forever. Therefore I do not run like a man <u>running</u> <u>aimlessly</u>; I do not fight like a man <u>beating</u> the air. No, I beat my body and make it a slave so that after I have preached to others, I myself will not be disqualified from the prize. (1 Corinthians 9:25-26 NIV)

Who serves as a soldier at his won expense? Who plants a <u>vineyard</u> and does not eat of its <u>grapes</u>? Who tends a flock and does not drink of the milk? Do not <u>muzzle</u> an ox while it is <u>treading</u> out the <u>grain</u>. If we have <u>sown</u> spiritual seed among you, is it too much if we reap a <u>material</u> harvest from you? In the same way, the Lord has commanded that those who preach the gospel should receive their living from the gospel.(I Corinthians 9:7, 9, 11, 14 NIV)

For <u>physical</u> training is of some value, but godliness has value for all things, <u>holding</u> promise for both the present life and the life to <u>come</u>. (1 Timothy 4:8 NIV)

```
I  M  I  T  C  C  A  F  F  A  I  R  S  C  R
N  A  R  R  S  R  I  R  U  N  N  I  N  G  C
V  T  H  A  B  E  O  V  E  D  P  V  A  O  H
O  E  C  I  E  M  M  P  I  E  B  I  M  S  O
L  R  A  N  A  U  X  A  S  L  M  E  N  T  L
V  I  L  I  T  Z  J  P  G  L  I  W  Z  R  D
E  A  A  N  I  Z  O  Q  E  C  O  A  G  I  I
D  L  C  G  N  L  S  S  O  R  S  N  N  C  N
V  S  I  I  G  E  S  M  C  J  W  E  W  T  G
I  M  S  L  T  L  P  G  F  B  Z  P  L  O  Y
C  L  Y  V  Y  E  R  G  R  A  P  E  S  U  S
T  Y  H  S  T  A  H  E  T  E  L  H  T  A  R
O  G  P  E  I  G  S  D  R  A  Y  E  N  I  V
R  I  S  N  X  N  T  G  N  I  D  A  E  R  T
S  O  L  D  I  E  R  P  I  H  S  D  R  A  H
```

76.Soldiers and Athletes

AFFAIRS	GAMES	RULES
AIMLESSLY	GRAIN	RUNNING
ATHLETE	GRAPES	SOLDIER
BEATING	HARDSHIP	SOWN
CIVILIAN	HOLDING	STRICT
COME	INVOLVED	TRAINING
COMPETES	MATERIAL	TREADING
CROPS	MUZZLE	VICTOR
CROWN	PHYSICAL	VINEYARD

77. Thanksgiving

And let the <u>peace</u> of God rule in your hearts, to the which also ye are called in one body; and be ye <u>thankful</u>. Let the word of Christ dwell in you <u>richly</u> in all wisdom; teaching and admonishing one another in <u>psalms</u> and <u>hymms</u> and spiritual <u>songs</u>, <u>singing</u> with <u>grace</u> in your hearts to the Lord. And whatsoever ye do in word or deed, do all in the name of the Lord Jesus, giving thanks to God and the Father by him. (Colossians 3:15-17 KJV)

Sing unto Lord with <u>thanksgiving</u>; sing praise upon the <u>harp</u> unto our God: Who <u>cover</u>eth the heaven with <u>clouds</u>, who prepareth <u>rain</u> for the earth, who maketh <u>grass</u> to grow upon the <u>mountains</u>. (Psalm 147:7-8 KJV)

Praise ye the Lord, O give thanks unto the Lord, for he is good: for his <u>mercy</u> endure<u>th</u> forever.

Save us, O Lord our God, and <u>gather</u> us from among the <u>heathen</u>, to give thanks unto thy holy name, and to <u>triumph</u> in thy praise. (Psalm 106:1, 47 KJV)

But give thanks be to God, which giveth us the victory through our Lord Jesus Christ. Therefore, my beloved brethen, be ye <u>steadfast</u>, unmovable, always abounding in the work of the Lord, forasmuch as ye know that your labor is not in <u>vain</u> in the Lord. (1 Corinthians 15:57-58 KJV)

Know ye that the Lord he is God: It is he that hath made us, and not we ourselves; we are his people, and the sheep of his <u>pasture</u>.

<u>Enter</u> into his <u>gates</u> with thanksgiving, and into his courts with praise: be thankful unto him, and bless his name. (Psalm 100:3-4 KJV)

And he took the <u>cup</u>, and gave thanks, and gave it to them, saying, "Drink ye all of it; For this is my blood of the new <u>testament</u>, which is <u>shed</u> for many for the remission of sins." (Matthew 26:27-28 KJV)

```
C U P T G R P G K E T H Y T S
B X F R E S A T R H Y J Q H T
T K A T A T R U A M V V Z A E
N C N L H I T N M D A D R N A
E E M E U S S O Y I N E K D
S S R M A G Z G D F N I C F F
I N P P I T R Y R Y U A A U A
Z H I V S C K I C A Y R E L S
J E I A H I L T C J S C P Y T
C N I J T E N O E H S S R B W
G J I I W N A G U S L E J E U
S H E D E K U T I D I Y T K M
H A R P U T H O H N S A D A Q
S O N G S M K Y M E G S R Z G
T E S T A M E N T T N V J P Y
```

77.Thanksgiving

CLOUDS	HYMMS	SHED
CUP	MERCY	SINGING
ENTER	MOUNTAINS	SONGS
GATES	PASTURE	STEADFAST
GATHER	PEACE	TESTAMENT
GRACE	PRAISE	THANKFUL
GRASS	PSALMS	THANSGIVING
HARP	RAIN	TRIUMPH
HEATHEN	RICHLY	VAIN

78. Ministry of Reconciliation

Since, then, we know what it is to <u>fear</u> the Lord, we try to <u>persuade</u> men. What we are is <u>plain</u> to God, and I hope it is also plain to your conscience. We are not <u>trying</u> to <u>commend</u> ourselves to you again, but are giving you an opportunity to <u>take</u> <u>pride</u> in us, so that you can <u>answer</u> those who take pride in what is seen <u>rather</u> than in what is in the heart. If we are out of our mind, it is for the sake of God; if we are in our mind, it is for you. For Christ's love <u>compels</u> us, because we are convinced that one <u>died</u> for all, and therefore all died. And he died for all, that those who live <u>should</u> no longer live for themselves but for him who died for them and was <u>raised</u> <u>again</u>.

So from now on we <u>regard</u> no one from a <u>worldly</u> <u>point</u> of <u>view</u>. Though we <u>once</u> regarded Christ in this way, we do no longer. Therefore, if anyone is in Christ he is a new <u>creation</u>, the old has gone, the <u>new</u> has come! All this is from God, who <u>reconciled</u> us to himself through Christ and gave us the <u>ministry</u> of reconciliation: that God was reconciling the world to himself in Christ, and not counting men's sins <u>against</u> them. And he committed to us the message of reconciliation. We are therefore Christ's <u>ambassadors,</u> as through us. We <u>implore</u> you on Christ's <u>behalf</u>: Be reconciled to God. God made him who had no sin to be sin for us, so that in him we might become the righteousness of God. (2 Corinthians 5:11-21 NIV)

```
P  R  A  D  P  E  R  S  U  A  D  E  S  E  S
A  L  E  N  E  J  E  R  O  L  P  M  I  R  B
X  V  A  G  S  L  A  G  A  I  N  W  O  Q  T
Q  V  V  I  A  W  I  O  N  C  E  D  A  N  A
Q  H  N  W  N  R  E  C  X  T  A  P  I  L  N
C  Y  D  O  Q  Q  D  R  N  S  C  O  G  X  E
N  R  N  R  D  I  E  D  S  O  P  L  K  C  W
O  T  E  L  N  E  S  A  B  D  C  H  M  D  J
I  S  M  D  W  W  B  E  R  T  E  E  R  T  W
T  I  M  L  K  M  H  A  D  M  R  S  R  O  F
A  N  O  Y  A  A  T  L  D  H  E  Y  I  R  E
E  I  C  V  L  H  U  T  A  K  E  D  I  A  A
R  M  X  F  E  O  V  I  E  W  D  R  I  N  R
C  L  Z  R  H  C  O  M  P  E  L  S  A  R  G
I  P  Q  S  P  O  J  T  S  N  I  A  G  A  P
```

78. Thanksgiving

AGAIN	FEAR	RAISED
AGAINST	IMPLORE	RATHER
AMBASSADORS	MINISTRY	RECONCILED
ANSWER	NEW	REGARD
BEHALF	ONCE	SHOULD
COMMEND	PERSUADE	TAKE
COMPELS	PLAIN	TRYING
CREATION	POINT	VIEW
DIED	PRIDE	WORLDLY

79. A Time for Everything

To everything there is a season,
And <u>time</u> to every purpose under the heaven:
A time to be <u>born</u>,
And a time to <u>die</u>;
A time to <u>plant</u>,
And a time to <u>pluck</u> up that which is planted;
A time to kill,
And a time to <u>heal</u>;
A time to <u>break</u> down,
And a time to <u>build up</u>;
A time to <u>weep</u>,
And a time to <u>laugh</u>;
A time to <u>mourn</u>,
And a time to <u>dance</u>;
A time to <u>cast away</u> stones,
And a time to <u>gather</u> <u>stones</u> <u>together</u>;
A time to <u>embrace</u>,
And a time to <u>refrain</u> from embracing;
A time to <u>get</u>,
And a time to <u>lose</u>;
A time to <u>keep</u>,
And a time to cast away;
A time to <u>rend</u>,
And a time to <u>sew</u>;
A time to keep <u>silence</u>,
And a time to <u>speak</u>;
A time to love,
And a time to <u>hate</u>;
A time of <u>war</u>,
And a time of peace.
(Ecclesiastes 3:1-8 KJV)

```
W  F  D  E  H  P  X  X  G  A  E  S  W  Z  N
R  E  S  E  L  H  B  M  T  M  I  A  A  B  A
O  O  A  A  G  R  P  O  B  L  D  G  R  K  B
L  L  N  U  E  Y  G  R  E  E  D  N  G  P  T
I  T  A  A  G  E  A  N  T  S  P  E  A  K  T
N  L  K  R  T  C  C  M  P  T  S  K  Q  W  P
Z  S  C  H  E  E  Y  Q  O  L  L  P  J  E  E
B  C  E  A  B  J  M  U  Y  U  U  H  E  S  E
U  R  L  Z  S  U  N  F  N  F  R  C  L  E  W
B  E  A  I  T  T  I  I  R  D  E  N  K  J  K
J  R  H  B  O  P  A  L  A  E  J  C  E  D  T
O  F  A  O  N  K  F  W  D  R  H  Y  N  H  Y
P  E  T  R  E  E  I  D  A  U  F  T  Q  A  M
B  E  E  N  S  E  M  I  T  Y  P  E  A  Q  D
R  E  N  D  E  Z  Y  F  R  T  E  G  R  G  O
```

79. A Time for Everything

BORN	HATE	REND
BREAK	HEAL	SEW
BUILDUP	KEEP	SILENCE
CASTAWAY	LAUGH	SPEAK
DANCE	LOSE	STONES
DIE	MOURN	TIME
EMBRACE	PLANT	TOGETHER
GATHER	PLUCK	WAR
GET	REFRAIN	WEEP

80. The Bread of Life

"Labor not for the meat which perisheth, but for that meat which endureth unto everlasting life, which the Son of Man shall give unto you: for him hath God the Father sealed... This is the work of God, that ye believe on him whom he hath sent... Verily, verily, I say unto you, Moses gave you not that bread from heaven, but my Father giveth you the true bread from heaven. For the bread of God is he which cometh down from heaven and giveth life unto the world... I am the bread of life: he that cometh to me shall never hunger; and he that believeth on me shall never thirst... Except ye eat the flesh of the Son of man, and drink his blood, ye have no life in you. Whoso eateth my flesh, and drinketh my blood, hath eternal life; and I will raise him up at the last day. For my flesh is meat indeed, and my blood is drink indeed." (John 6:27, 32-33, 35, 53-55 KJV)

" I have meat to eat that ye know not of... My meat is to do the will of him that sent me, and to finish his work." (John 4:32 KJV)

For I have received of the Lord that which also I delivered unto you, That the Lord Jesus the same night in which he was betrayed took bread: And when he had given thanks, he brake it, and said, "Take, eat: this is my body, which is broken for you: this do in remembrance of me. After the same manner also he took the cup, when he had supped, saying, "This cup is the new testament in my blood: this do ye, as oft as ye drink it, in remembrance of me." For as often as ye eat this bread, and drink this cup, ye do show the Lord's death till he come. (1 Corinthians 11:23-26 KJV)

```
G S B N S E N T Q J M K I D J
I S U R E F R W D K J T A D F
V A K P A T S U T T H E E C W
E M L N P K F Z E G R L R U E
C E J Q E E E O I B A E D P R
P D D I Q K D N D E G W I V Q
Y W H O S O O O S N J E S U S
L L A H S L O R U D L O V E S
T J E G E L P H B Y E Y O U U
M Y A S B T M X G O L A M N P
L A I J S A V E O L M I T E T
B A K R N D V Q A W T R R H H
R V I N Z M O S H O U I E E E
B H E M E A T O O E S V T K V
T R C L G B M K O H E V A G L
```

Copyright □ GIL PUBLICATIONS 2004

80. Bread of Life

BLOOD	LAST	SENT
BRAKE	MANNER	SHALL
BREAD	MEAT	SUPPED
BROKEN	NIGHT	THIRST
CUP	OFTEN	TOOK
DEATH	PERISH	TRUE
GAVE	RAISE	VERILY
GIVE	SAME	WHOM
HUNGER	SEALED	WHOSO

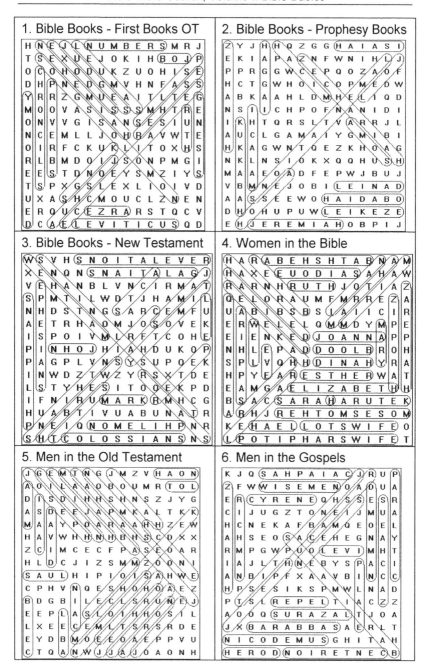

1. Bible Books - First Books OT

2. Bible Books - Prophesy Books

3. Bible Books - New Testament

4. Women in the Bible

5. Men in the Old Testament

6. Men in the Gospels

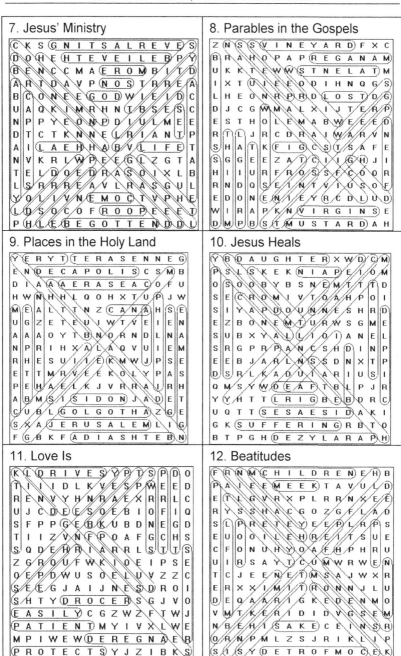

7. Jesus' Ministry

8. Parables in the Gospels

9. Places in the Holy Land

10. Jesus Heals

11. Love Is

12. Beatitudes

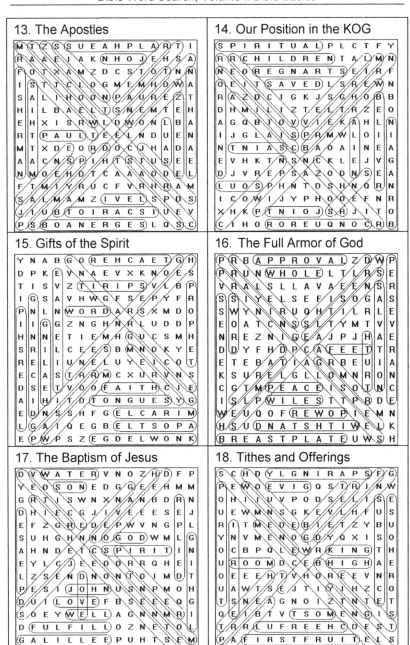

13. The Apostles

14. Our Position in the KOG

15. Gifts of the Spirit

16. The Full Armor of God

17. The Baptism of Jesus

18. Tithes and Offerings

19. Humility
20. Devils, Demons, Fallen Angels
21. Hebrews in the Wilderness
22. Hebrews Tested in the Desert
23. Jesus Tempted in the Desert
24. Prayer

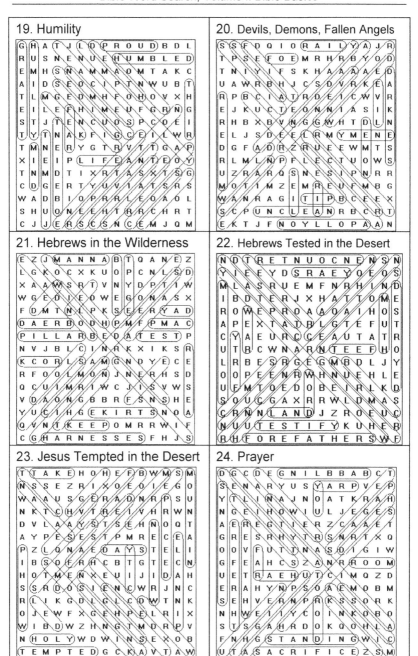

25. Faith

26. The Fall of Jericho

27. Prosperity

28. Pharisees

29. Tongue

30. Seed

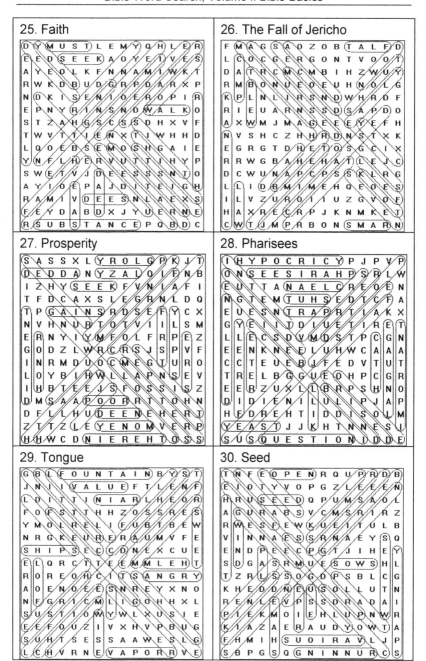

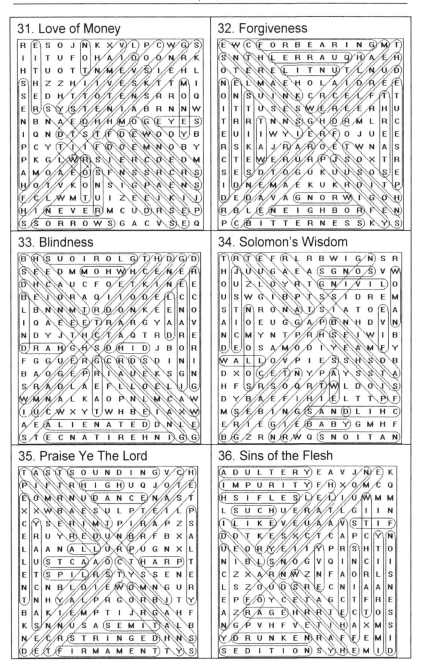

31. Love of Money

32. Forgiveness

33. Blindness

34. Solomon's Wisdom

35. Praise Ye The Lord

36. Sins of the Flesh

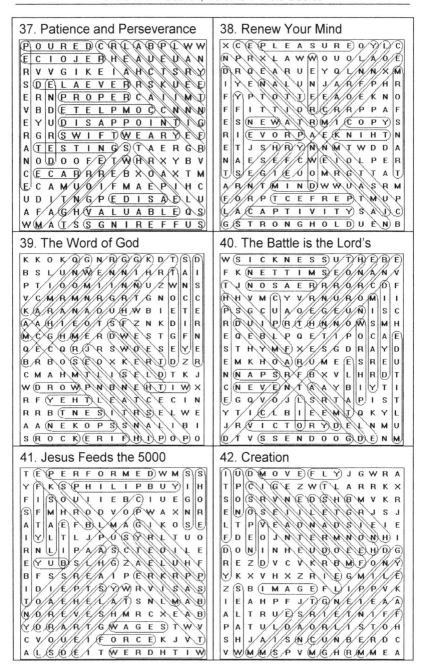

37. Patience and Perseverance

38. Renew Your Mind

39. The Word of God

40. The Battle is the Lord's

41. Jesus Feeds the 5000

42. Creation

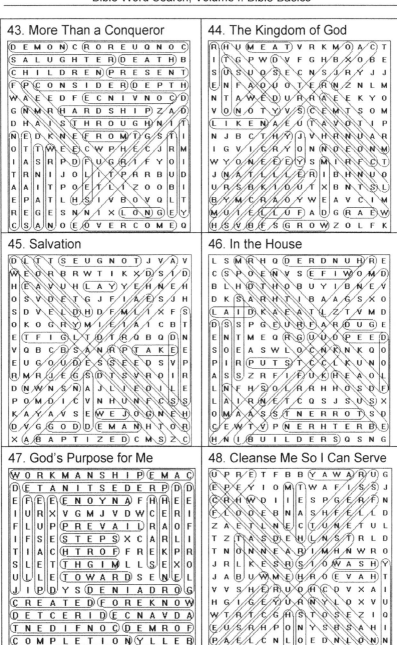

43. More Than a Conqueror

44. The Kingdom of God

45. Salvation

46. In the House

47. God's Purpose for Me

48. Cleanse Me So I Can Serve

49. The Flood - Noah

50. Please God Not Man

51. God's Power For Us

52. Freedom in Christ

53. Do Not Worry

54. Rest for Your Souls

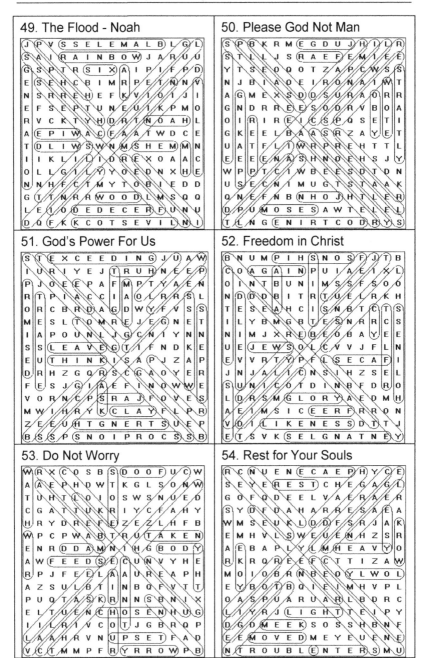

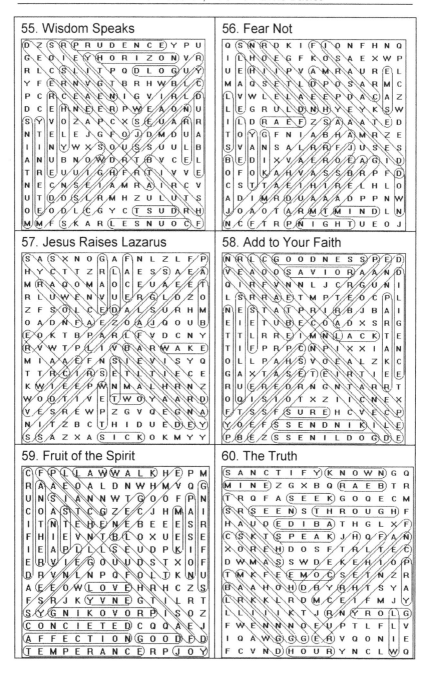

55. Wisdom Speaks

56. Fear Not

57. Jesus Raises Lazarus

58. Add to Your Faith

59. Fruit of the Spirit

60. The Truth

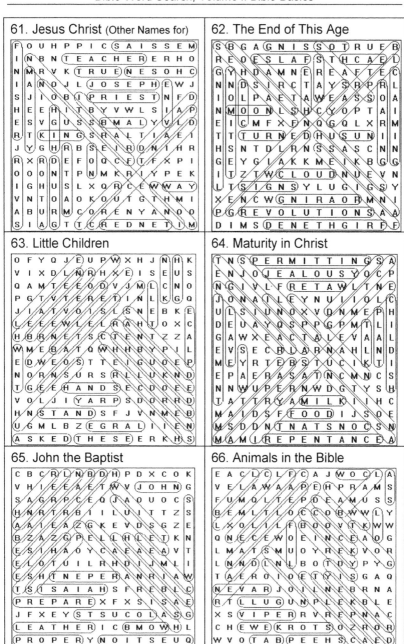

61. Jesus Christ (Other Names for)

62. The End of This Age

63. Little Children

64. Maturity in Christ

65. John the Baptist

66. Animals in the Bible

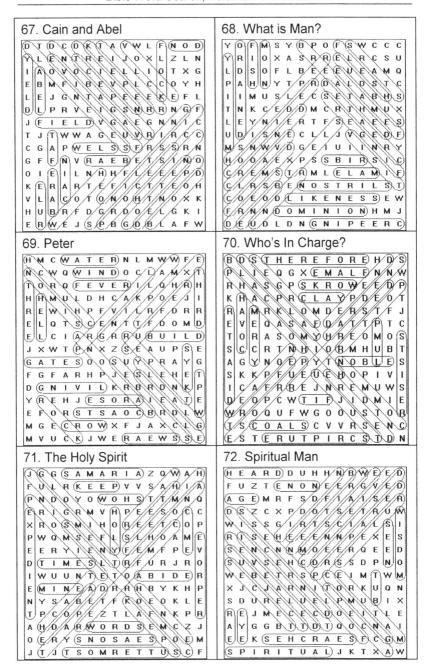

67. Cain and Abel

68. What is Man?

69. Peter

70. Who's In Charge?

71. The Holy Spirit

72. Spiritual Man

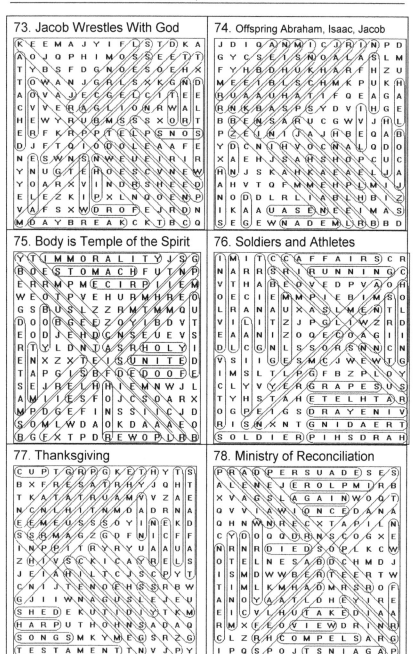

73. Jacob Wrestles With God

74. Offspring Abraham, Isaac, Jacob

75. Body is Temple of the Spirit

76. Soldiers and Athletes

77. Thanksgiving

78. Ministry of Reconciliation

79. A Time for Everything

```
W F D E H P X X G A E S W Z N
R E S E H B M T M A A B A
O O A A G R P O B L D G R K B
L L N U E Y G R E E D N G P T
I T A A G E A N T S P E A K T
N L K A T C C M P T S K Q W P
Z S C H E E Y O O L L P J E E
B C E A B J M U Y U U H E S E
U R L Z S U N F N F R C L E W
B E A I T T I I R D E N K J K
J R H B O P A L A E J C E D T
O F A O N K F W D R H Y N H Y
P E T R E E I D A U F T Q A M
B E E N S E M I T Y P E A Q D
R E N D E Z Y F R T E G R G O
```

80. The Bread of Life

```
G S B N S E N T Q J M K I D J
I S U R E F R W D K J T A D F
V A K P A T S U T T H E E C W
E M L N P K F Z E G R L R U E
C E J O E E E O I B A E D P R
P D D I O K D N D E G W I V Q
Y W H O S O O O S N J E S U S
L L A H S L O R U D L O V E S
T J E G E L P H B Y E Y O U U
M Y A S B T M X G O L A M N P
L A I J S A V E O L M I D E T
B A K R N D V Q A W T R A H H
R V I N Z M O S H O U I E E E
B H E M E A T O O E S V T K V
T B C L G B M K O H E V A G L
```

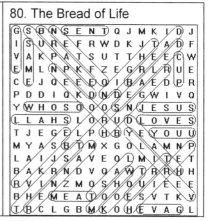

Can You Solve This Puzzle?

100-Word Bible Word Search Poster #1
"God's Word – A Lamp Unto My Feet"

Hidden Message:

Scriptures

FREE GIFT
100-Word
Bible Word Search
Poster #1
(with Hidden Message)

"God's Word –
A Lamp Unto My Feet"

Send a Self-Addressed Stamped Envelope to:
G.I.L. PUBLICATIONS
P. O. Box 80275, Brooklyn, NY 11208

GIL Publications, P. O. Box 80275, Brooklyn, NY 11208
www.BibleWordSearchPuzzles.com

Do You Have a Relationship With God?

The Bible tells us that:

... if you confess with your mouth, "Jesus is Lord," and believe in your heart that God raised him from the dead, you will be saved.

Romans 10:9 KJV

HAVE YOU ACCEPTED JESUS AS YOUR LORD?

If you do not have a relationship with God – through accepting Jesus as Lord – then I invite you to please pray the following prayer:

> *Lord, I come before you today to confess that I accept Jesus as my Lord and Savior and that I believe you raised Him from the dead. I believe that He died for my sins and that only through Him can I be saved.*
>
> *Lord, please forgive me of all my sins and accept me into your Kingdom. Lord, I welcome the Holy Spirit into my heart today.*
>
> *I thank you, Lord, in Jesus' Name, Amen.*

Congratulations! Now, you - as a born-again Christian can best maintain your walk with God by:

- Praying daily – ask God to help you with the challenges in your life and to bring you closer to Himself
- Read and Study God's Word (the Bible) daily
- Attend a Bible teaching church
- Fellowship with other serious Christians

A good place to start your Bible reading is with the book of John.

If you have questions or need help please write to me at:

Akili Kumasi
GOD IS LOVE MINISTRIES
P.O. Box 80275, Brooklyn, NY 11208
kumasi@GILpublications.com

Mail Order ....GIL Publications
                         P. O. Box 80275, Brooklyn, NY 11208
Telephone Orders...............(718) 386-6434
Website Orders ....www.GILpublications.com

SCRIPTURE REFERENCE BOOKS			
Book Title	**Price**	**#**	**Total**
God's Healing Scriptures 240 Prayers & Promises in the Bible	$9.95		
101 Women in the Bible	$6.95		
101 Prayers in the Bible	$6.95		
101 Victories in the Bible	$6.95		
HALL OF FAITH CLASSICS			
Volume 1: The Person and Work of the Holy Spirit (R.A. Torrey)	$9.75		
Volume 2: How to Pray (R.A. Torrey)	$5.95		
Volume 3: How To Obtain the Fullness of Power for Life and Christian Service (R.A. Torrey)	$5.75		
Volume 4: Absolute Surrender (Andrew Murray)	$6.25		
Volume 5: Humility: The Beauty of Holiness (Andrew Murray)	$5.75		
Hall of Faith 5-Pack (Volumes 1, 2, 3, 4, 5) - $25% off – Save $8.35	$25.10		
FATHERHOOD BOOKS			
Fatherhood Principles of Joseph the Carpenter	$8.95		
Fun Meals for Fathers and Sons	$4.95		
On the Outside Looking In	$7.95		

To pay by Credit / Debit Card – go to www.GILpublications.com or call 718-386-6434

Complete the Order Form on the next page

Mail Order .... GIL Publications
                                      P. O. Box 80275, Brooklyn, NY 11208
Telephone Orders .... (718) 386-6434
Website Orders .... www.GILpublications.com

Book Title	Price	#	Total
Bible Word Search – Puzzles with Scriptures (80 puzzles per book)			
Vol. I: **Extracts** from the Bible	$7.95		
Vol. II: **Women** in the Bible	$7.95		
Vol. III: **Fathers** in the Bible	$7.95		
Vol. IV: **Prayers** in the Bible	$7.95		
Vol. V: **Victories** in the Bible	$7.95		
Vol. VI: **Parables** in the Bible	$7.95		
Vol. VII: **Promises** in the Bible	$7.95		
Vol. VIII: **Foundations** in Christianity **(100 Puzzles)**	$8.95		
Bible Word Search 8-Pack (all 8 books) *– 17% off – Save $11.00*	$53.62		
Bible Word Search, **Large Print, No. 1**	$5.95		
Church Edition CD - *560 puzzles –* (7 volumes, lesson plans, group activities)	$5.95		
EDUCATOR'S WORD SEARCH Vol. 1: U.S. Presidents	$5.95		
	Sub-Total		
	NY Residents Add 8.5% Tax		
	Shipping ($3.95 1st item, 50¢ each additional)		
	TOTAL		

Date:_____ Payment: ☒ Check ☒ Money Order
Name:_____
Address:_____
City:_____ State:_____ Zip:_____
Telephone:_____
E-Mail:_____

Made in the USA
Middletown, DE
17 December 2020